Understanding the Secret Language of Money

Why most Americans are unaware of the ways successful people think, communicate and behave when it comes to finance and money related decisions

ISBN: 0615958826

ISBN 13: 978-0615958828

Contents

Section I—Diagnosing the Problem

Section II—Developing the Solution

Section II—Developing the Solution (continued)

ABOUT THE AUTHOR

John E. Moriarty has been an entrepreneur in the wealth management industry since 1995. John is the founder and president of E3 Consultants Group, a comprehensive wealth management firm he started in 2003 with a unique business model focused on creating value for clients in finance and money related areas. His passion for personal service is reflected in E3's integrated resource network of financial professionals who help clients take control of their financial picture and protect their personal economy.

John is an investment advisor representative in the State of Missouri and is a designated Chartered Financial Consultant (ChFC). He has passed several securities industry exams including the Series 7, 22, 24, 63 and 65 licenses. In addition, John is an Office of Supervisory Jurisdiction (OSJ) Manager, and a licensed broker for both health and life insurance in several states.

John graduated summa cum laude as the top finance student from Saint Louis University with a BSBA in Finance (1996) while also pitching for SLU's baseball team his entire college career. He is a member of several nationally recognized financial service organizations, including the Financial Planning Association (FPA), National Association of Insurance and Financial Advisors (NAIFA) and the Society of Financial Services Professionals. John is also a member of the Entrepreneur Organization (EO) – St. Louis Chapter which brings local entrepreneurs together to improve their business models.

Educating the public is essential in today's economy, so John hosts a weekly radio show called "Maximize Your Money" that can be heard every Saturday 2:00-3:00pm on KFTK 97.1 FM in St. Louis, MO.

Born and raised in St. Louis, John currently resides in Webster Groves, MO with his wife, Ellen and their two children, Harrison and Catherine. Growing up in "baseball heaven" has made the entire family huge St. Louis Cardinal fans and in his free time, John is an avid golfer as well as a wine and cigar enthusiast.

If you would like to contact John directly, you can do so in the following manner:
E3 Consultants Group
10825 Watson Road, Suite 100. Sunset Hills, MO 63127
Office: 314.822.4440 and Email: jmoriarty@e3wealth.com
www.e3wealth.com
www.advanceandprotect.com

DISCLAIMER

Providing financial guidance to the public is challenging. It becomes more challenging as you begin to factor in things such as individual needs and wants. This is compounded by variables such as unique personal circumstances and ever-changing regulations. This book reflects the author's opinions, which are not endorsed by National Planning Corporation (the author's broker-dealer). These opinions are not intended to provide specific advice and should not be construed as recommendations for any individual. This book is published with the understanding that the author is not engaged in rendering legal or tax services. Investments involve risk including the potential for loss of the principal amount invested. Past performance is no guarantee of future results. Please remember that investment decisions should be based on an individual's goals, time horizon and tolerance for risk. The services of competent legal, tax and financial professionals should be sought prior to executing any strategy. All examples provided are hypothetical in nature and are intended for informational purposes only.

FOREWORD

To the entrepreneur in all of us. May this book educate,
empower, and enlighten you toward financial freedom.

When I started creating the content for this book, my intention was to touch, move, impact, or agitate you, the reader, enough to change your perspective on finance and money related decisions. Some parts of this book may make you feel uneasy. If so, I encourage you to keep reading because you could be nearing a breakthrough. It's very possible to experience several different emotions as you digest the material in this book: curiosity, fear, anger, excitement, or even relief. This process needs to occur so that you can uncover your limiting beliefs. Once you realize what is standing between you and financial security then you can identify the resources and services that can add value to your financial life.

My passion in business is to awaken the inner entrepreneur in all of us. The entrepreneurial mindset is present when individuals, families, and small business owners do the following:

- *Educate* themselves on financial topics that protect their personal economies
- *Gain confidence* in their minds that financial freedom is attainable for them
- *Take action* toward customized, one-sized-fits-one solutions through proactive implementation of cutting-edge strategies
- *Establish trust* with a team of resources that properly manage expectations
- *Adjust* their paths as the world around them changes

Why do I find this entrepreneurial awakening so important? I believe that there are real economic forces working against individuals, families, and small business owners who have saver mentalities because they contradict our consumer-driven society. I am not saying these forces are evil or intend to harm the average American, but I do believe that certain elements of our society benefit from the effects of consumerism. Also, I don't want readers to think that this book is only for business owners or entrepreneurs. I believe that you can have financial success regardless of occupation, current age, income, upbringing, or level of education. You will uncover the key to your success as you understand your relationship with money and the habits you have formed over time. Your beliefs about finance are built over many years of experiences. They start when you are a young child

1

through adolescence into adulthood, culminating in your golden years. The ability to uncover your habits and relationship with money is a skill most financial professionals do not even possess.

What differentiates our firm, E3 Consultants Group, from every other financial service organization in the country is how we use the science of neuro-linguistic programming (NLP). E3 is a comprehensive wealth management firm I started in 2003 that serves individuals, families, and small businesses interested in a different approach to finance and money related decisions. The science of NLP demystifies the link among the mindset, language, and behavior of any human being. NLP is a tool to unlock the clues to where you are right now in your relationship with money and helps solidify our firm's role in adding value to your financial future. Keep this in mind as you proceed, and I hope you can see why I want to proactively challenge the way Americans are educated about finance and money related decisions.

INTRODUCTION

Writing this book has been part of my never ending journey to explain my perspective on money and the different ways to use it properly. I see no end in sight for this journey because the need for financial literacy has increased substantially since 2008. The core issues of our collective problem have developed over decades, causing the majority of Americans to build a poor relationship with money. Our country was founded on the entrepreneurial ambitions of pioneers searching for a new way of life. The status quo maintained by the lifestyle in their previous land stifled ingenuity, independence, and personal freedoms. This was reason enough to venture across an ocean to an unknown land and start new lives.

I believe our society is at a similar point today as the US government, the Federal Reserve, corporations, financial institutions, and the media continually attack the middle class. I simply can no longer sit by and watch my children's (and possibly grandchildren's) futures be confiscated through the mishandling of our nation's currency and economic resources. It is time for a new age of enlightenment, and it must take place through responsibility for one's personal economy. While the mission may seem impossible, I am confident that the risks to our way of life are much greater if we sit back and do nothing, essentially allowing an entitlement society to overtake our ability to succeed or fail on our own merits.

How do you get started on this new journey? I believe that you first need to understand the causes of our predicament and the forces working against your wellbeing. Then you can equip yourself with the knowledge and strategies to protect your personal economy and finally take control of your financial picture, with this book as your guide. If you believe its message accurately depicts our current dilemma then my firm's methods are in alignment with your thought process. Our desire is to build a movement of like-minded people who want to work together to make this country a great nation once again. The most difficult step toward that goal is first realizing what a mess we are currently in and the desire to change our direction.

As we diagnose the problem, the reality of our situation will become clearer. Our citizenry's fiscal dependence on others is found in the areas of society where governmental control is rampant: education, housing, banking, retirement, and employment. When you start to understand the gradual deterioration of these areas over the last forty years then you can comprehend the motivation behind the difficult financial decisions you must make throughout your lifetime. You don't make

3

those decisions in a vacuum. Generations of families are taught to believe certain myths about money, and they pass those "lessons" down to their children. We need a generation of Americans to break the cycle of financial illiteracy and gain true knowledge about everyone's human resources (time, talent, and capital). It is then that protecting personal economy is possible for those who value financial independence and control over their economic futures.

Once people wake up and decide that they are ready to take control of their financial pictures, following a process and philosophy that empowers each of us toward first-generation wealth is key. I've been working toward this goal for myself and my family every day of my entrepreneurial career. Ever since I realized the awesome opportunities this country provides someone who is disciplined, driven, and focused on creating value, I've wanted to share this vision with whoever was interested.

I did not grow up with money. As the oldest child of a Saint Louis city policeman and a stay-at-home mom raising four kids, I knew that survival was more of a priority than accumulating material possessions. Being blessed with a knack for good grades and playing sports, I could excel in areas of life that offered an escape route from our financial realities. I attended an academically strong, private Jesuit high school, finishing in the top 5 percent of my class while playing varsity basketball and baseball. Then I moved on to Saint Louis University, where I graduated summa cum laude as the top finance student in my class while playing Division I college baseball. But while my personal successes were just beginning, the rest of my family was struggling. My parents divorced while I was in high school, and we almost lost our home due to my father's gambling problems; he was always thinking he could "win" the shortfall in the household budget. Money had always been an issue in our household, and the topic created an uneasy tension that made even sitting at the dinner table most nights unbearable. My parents had struggled to find money for home repairs, kids' activities, school tuition, car troubles, groceries, braces for our teeth, and just enough to pay that month's bills.

I knew a lot of families who were in the same situation, but for some reason, I never felt poor or disadvantaged myself. I had a lot of great friends, and most of my days were spent playing sports in other kids' backyards or hanging out at their homes. Experiencing other home environments gave me different perspectives on how other families talked about the topic of money in their households.

Additionally, I was blessed to have a few guardian angels looking out for me, providing me guidance throughout my early life. My grandfather Arthur "Art" Schmittgens did so much for me that I made sure every day that he was proud to call me his grandson. His influence was simple—he taught me the life lessons he learned in the military and as a father of six children. He gave me unconditional love but made sure I knew he had high expectations. He was always a presence, whether he was at one of my sporting events or we were out in public or just watching TV. Art was a man of few words, so when he spoke, it carried a lot of weight. He started a family in an era when our country was full of hope and optimism—the 1950s through early 1960s. Art worked for the same company for more than thirty years and believed that the United States of America was the greatest nation on earth because we all had the opportunity to chase our dreams. I mention these things because if my grandfather were alive today, his perspective on this country would most likely be a mix of anger and sorrow at how far we have strayed from that greatness. This book is my attempt to get us back on track and continue to make Art proud of my daily actions.

The other person who made a profound impact on my life was Larry Nance. Larry was the father of one of my good friends with whom I played baseball all through high school and college. Mr. Nance and his wife, Jane, came from the same background as my parents, growing up not too far from one another. The Nance's had four kids, just like us, and gave them the exact same educational opportunities that my family received. But the thing that set the Nance family apart and put them on a different trajectory was that Mr. Nance started his own business early in life and created an environment of first-generation wealth for his family and anyone around them willing to learn. Larry and Jane built their business from Larry selling products out of the trunk of his car to where it is today—a leader in its industry and a family business run by the Nance's children.

Mr. Nance's love for business could only be matched by his passion for sports. When his boys got to the age when competitive summer teams were a common goal for aspiring baseball players, it was only fitting that Larry start a selective summer baseball team with his sons as part of its nucleus—the Saint Louis Sabres.

And Larry's entrepreneurial spirit could not allow this to be an ordinary summer team—the select few who made the squad were given big-league treatment. Playing on a team with multiple uniforms that traveled across the country to play the best teams anywhere was incredible. We stayed in really nice hotels and ate like kings. The first real steak I ever had was on a team road trip. I never knew meat could taste so good. At the ages of sixteen to eighteen, most of the twenty-five young men on the roster were getting to experience life through an abundance mindset for the first time. The Nance's even gave us summer jobs at their factory because they didn't want us to lose our employment because of out-of-town tournaments.

For some people today, this type of travel and elite sports competition is commonplace. But what set our experiences apart was that the Nance's paid for 100 percent of all costs associated with the team: uniforms, travel, lodging, food, and equipment. You name it, they paid for it. This opportunity had a profound and lasting impact on my psyche. In fact, Larry and Jane Nance took their small business success and translated it into an entrepreneurial environment that changed my future. For this reason, the Nance family will always have a special place in my heart.

What if more families could share *or* experience this type of abundance? It doesn't need to involve just sports, either. Giving kids the opportunity to succeed in any area of life that makes them happy is essential to my book's message. One thing all parents want is for their children to have better lives than the ones they led. How can this desire be achieved with today's economic uncertainty and misguided financial principles? If you are willing to take the time to read this book, I am confident that you will find the answers to these questions and many more you may have about ways to use and maintain control over your money.

Educate. Empower. Enlighten.

Chapter 1: The Era of Financial Dependence on the Status Quo

To fully comprehend the economic and societal problems we face as a country because of misperceptions regarding finances, one must first grasp the magnitude of our collective actions over the past hundred years. The vast majority of Americans have forgotten that the most important characteristics of a good financial picture are *flexibility* and *control*—because they give you the personal freedom to *choose*. That freedom has been lost (some would say stolen) by the government's actions over the last hundred years, especially the two big ones in 1913:

- o Introduction of the federal income tax
- o Creation of the Federal Reserve

These two actions allowed the government to slowly take control over the value of our currency and shape the way we make financial decisions. Ultimately, *the state wants you to believe that it can do better for you than you can for yourself*, and the vehicle that produces this "utopia" is the redistribution of wealth through taxes and inflation. The state maintains our society's status quo by relying on other entities besides ourselves for creativity and innovation. Its empty promises are a driving force behind the current mess we are in. Don't just look at the "fiscal cliff" (budget deficits and debt). Expand your perspective into all of the areas in which our government has created problems (or has perpetuated them) due to our country's lack of entrepreneurial drive:

- Education
- Housing
- Banking
- Employment
- Retirement

Education

Have you ever wondered where the phrase "knowledge is power" originated? This simple three-word sentence encapsulates the true purpose of this book. Knowledge can be defined as information and skills acquired through experience or education. Power can be defined as the ability to do something or act in a particular way. Similar words to the noun *power* are might, force, strength, potency, authority, and energy. So knowledge equals education, and power comes from your ability to turn that education into action.

Ultimately, your financial power comes from taking control of your own financial picture. Of course, today's economic uncertainty has made such a process seem almost impossible. Mistrust of the government, the banking system, and Wall Street has led millions of savers in this country to seriously doubt themselves. The fear of making the wrong decision is causing people to make *no* decisions about where they should invest their hard-earned life savings. This *crisis of confidence* manifests itself in several areas of the economy: housing, employment, banking, investing, politics, and business, to name a few. What are average Americans supposed to do?

Knowledge is power, and it all starts with *education*. Expand your knowledge beyond what you know that *most people do with their money*. Create certainty with a mindset that fits *your* needs and wants. Unfortunately, our society's educational system has deteriorated over the past several decades. When the effects of this are coupled with the rising costs of private elementary, high school, college, and postgraduate degrees, the *value* of education goes down.

Over the past thirty years, the modern workplace has radically changed, and the demands on those transitioning from classroom to workforce continue to rise. Students from Birmingham and Boston no longer compete against each other for jobs; instead, their rivals are well-educated students from Sydney and Singapore. But as globalization has progressed, America's educational progress has stagnated. Today, the United States' high school graduation rate ranks near the bottom among developed nations belonging to the Organisation for Economic Co-Operation and Development (OECD).[1] In fact, the United States has substantial inequities in achievement across the country, and the performance gap between the most- and least-proficient students here is among the highest of all OECD countries.

The following details how fifteen-year-old American students compare with fifteen-year-olds in other OECD member countries in the Programme for International Student Achievement (PISA) measures of academic proficiency. The United States ranked among OECD countries in:

---

[1] Alliance for Excellent Education, Fact Sheet, "How Does the United States Stack Up?" March 2008, www.all4ed.org

Reading literacy
- fifteenth of 29 in 2003
- fourteenth of 34 in 2010

Scientific literacy
- twenty-first of 30 in 2003
- seventeenth of 34 in 2010

Mathematics literacy
- twenty-fifth of 30 in 2003
- twenty-fifth of 34 in 2010

Our country is the only OECD member to have relatively high proportions of both top and bottom performers (OECD 2007b); we have an average number of students who perform at the highest proficiency levels but a much larger proportion who perform at the lowest.

Why is this happening? The choices for a good education are now based on geography and finances. Good public schools versus bad public schools—or pay for private education. If you believe a good education is the foundation of a developing society then we are falling behind.

The quality of our educational system can be considered poor when the investment of time and capital are factored in. The time spent in organized education for most Americans wanting a "better" life for themselves is about nineteen to twenty-two years:

- nine years in elementary school
- four years in high school
- four to five years in college
- two to four years for a postgraduate degree

What are the career prospects in today's society for those who commit to twenty years of school (and whose parents invest potentially hundreds of thousands of dollars on that education)? So many struggle to find jobs in their fields of study, but even thousands of college graduates are unable to find *any* job. It is very possible that the skill sets that they build over two decades of schooling prepare them inadequately for our current economy. Why, in twenty years of formal education, is there no real focus on providing financial literacy?

Improving your understanding of simple money principles is a core purpose of this book. I will show you:

- How balancing your needs and wants starts with good cash flow management
- How creating a spending awareness builds good habits, leading to appropriate spending on housing and transportation
- Why it is important to pay yourself first (i.e., save) but also how it is possible to do so
- How to avoid the debt trap by understanding the benefits of delayed gratification

Ask yourself: who (and what systems) *benefits* from a citizen's lack of financial knowledge?

Housing

How many times have you heard someone say that one of the most fundamental elements to a good life is owning your own home? The house you own, however, should be one you can *afford*. Home affordability has been severely damaged since real incomes have stagnated for almost forty years.

How has our government responded to its citizens' financial woes? When people lost their homes and farms during the Great Depression, it created institutions that aimed to make sure that wouldn't happen again. These were Fannie Mae and Freddie Mac, government-backed but private, for-profit companies. Their jobs are to set lending standards for our banking system and to stand behind them with guarantees. They help securitize loans as an investment for the bond market. But here's a good question to ask yourself: when a for-profit company has government guarantees behind it, is it more concerned about minimizing risk or maximizing profit? If the companies make money, the shareholders and executives win. But if they lose money and fail, the taxpayer bails them out. And you know the rest of the story based on our recent housing market.

The government has wanted to keep increasing home ownership, fostering the idea of the American dream, but standards on loans decreased during the first half of the 2000s, allowing people to believe they could afford homes that they could not. Fannie Mae, Freddie Mac, Wall Street, and other companies in the housing market, plus real estate speculators, made a fortune until the bubble burst in 2006, when hundreds of billions of dollars were needed for bailouts, millions of jobs were lost, trillions of dollars in phantom wealth were erased, and millions of homes were foreclosed on. It took the housing market six years just to get back to "recovery" mode. But millions of people have ruined credit and bleak financial pictures. How is this the American dream?

Whether you have achieved financial success should not be determined by whether you rent or own your home. Home ownership has a number of financial and emotional advantages (from tax benefits to creating memories with your family), but your priority must be *affordability*. What you can afford depends on several variables: your income, your credit history, the size of your family, your desired location, and the state of the economy. Depending on where the interest rate market is at that time, renting versus buying is a decision that can have a long-term impact on your financial picture. Since very few people can buy a home with 100 percent cash, borrowing money from a bank becomes a necessity. Structuring the terms of the loan so that they benefit you as well as the bank is all about *controlling the flow of your money*—which is the American dream I subscribe to based on today's economic uncertainty.

Banking

The problems that arose from the housing bubble shined a big, bright light on our banking industry and its faults. Before we go into those problems, let's discuss the role of banking in our economy.

Why do banks exist? What is their function in our economy? If you are a *saver*, a bank is a place where you deposit funds that you want to keep safe and liquid (through savings accounts or certificates of deposit) and earn a decent interest rate on (so you can stay ahead of taxes and inflation). If you need to *borrow* funds for consumer purchases (home, car, boat, or education), the bank lends you funds at a market rate of interest because you have not saved enough money to pay cash. This is a key aspect to our capitalistic economy: credit.

If you are a *business*, a bank is a source of capital for both operations and expansion. Without a source of capital, a business could struggle, miss growth opportunities, and hold back on hiring new employees. A good bank is profitable when it earns a good *spread* on the interest rates paid to savers versus interest rates earned from borrowers. A good bank focuses on taking less risk and building relationships with its customers so that it can understand their habits.

So why is the banking system so fouled up? Banking systems date back centuries. The one we know today, the Federal Reserve system, was established a hundred years ago in 1913. All modern-day bankers and most citizens have been born into this present system. Unfortunately, as a society, we've been very naïve about the current financial system and the way it allows commercial banks to literally create money out of thin air for the benefit of their owners (major banks) and major customers (the US Treasury).

The Federal Reserve has created its own role in our "fractional reserve" banking system, where in for every ten dollars deposited, only one dollar goes into reserves, while the other nine dollars can be loaned out. Banks are leveraging your savings to make money. The Federal Reserve is the vehicle in our system that creates money *out of thin air.* Banks have become more focused on profits as our economy has fallen in love with debt. The more rewards they earned from the risks they took, the more leverage they added to their balance sheet (it is said that at the time when Lehman Brothers went bankrupt, its balance sheet was leveraged forty to one). Deposit-holding banks became "investment banks" and got "too big to fail." We spent the years between 2008 and 2013 helping the banks heal their own balance sheets on the backs of savers.

Now this system is helping finance our government deficits. The Federal Reserve is *monetizing* our country's debt by increasing its balance sheet. Right now, the Fed is buying the debt that the US Treasury is bringing to the market through quantitative easing (QE) programs.

How will the US government ever pay off this debt? My opinion is that it will *inflate* it away and ruin the *real value* of assets owned by its citizens. As the value of the dollar decreases, the debt becomes *cheaper* and easier to pay off with new money the government creates. Anyone holding dollars (or assets valued in dollars) will become a victim of this legal charade.

Most people are oblivious to the long-term negative effects our current banking system generates through its daily operations. But your hard-earned savings no longer earn you much of anything when you store your money at the bank. This causes frustration to mount in a true saver, which is compounded by our struggling employment market.

Employment

This country was founded by *entrepreneurs*. People came to this country to experience a new beginning—what came to be known as the American dream. Nothing was owed to a citizen; no one was entitled to anything. All one expected was the opportunity to achieve whatever his or her talents would allow. Essentially, this was the chance to be an entrepreneur.

Entrepreneurship is "the process in which one or more people undertake economic risk to create a new organization that will exploit a new technology or innovative process that generates values for others."[2] Entrepreneurship is a mindset. The trick is to educate and encourage the largest number of people to feel comfortable with the notion that they can start businesses, control their destinies, and contribute to society through innovation and hard work. At any given time, 15 percent of the population is running its own companies. Our goal should be to make starting a business as common as getting married or parenting.[3]

But just as we experienced the joys of capitalism, we also suffered from the side effects of greed and excess. After the Great Depression, people were taught to rely for security on the government more and more and less on themselves. Keynesian economics was upheld as a way to smooth out the business cycle so people didn't have to go through as much pain in recessions. So the government would spend when the private sector couldn't or wouldn't. This government spending would accelerate in the 1970s, when we permanently went off the gold standard. As we entered the 1990s and 2000s, we started to have *jobless recoveries,* where the private sector did not hire people back, but the public sector (the government) picked up the slack.

---

[2] Carl J. Schramm, *The Entrepreneurial Imperative: How America's Economic Miracle Will Reshape the World (and Change Your Life)*, 4
[3] Schramm, *Entrepreneurial Imperative*, 11

So what are the consequences? More people become *public sector* employees (in federal, state, and local governments), and the government's payroll expenses grow larger, impacting society in several ways:

- People become dependent on the government.
- Government needs to increase its budget (*deficit* grows).
- Government either taxes more or prints more money (*debt* grows).
- We become dependent on other countries to finance our society.
- When other countries won't buy our debt, we buy it ourselves (through the Federal Reserve).

We've been offered $17 trillion in promises, and people are poorly educated with their homes worth less. There's no trust in banks or Wall Street; people are not prepared for retirement and are worried about their jobs. Does that sound like a utopia?

Please realize that I am not saying that being a public employee is *bad*. But people need to understand how the government has been involved in creating our current entitlement society. We need entrepreneurs to start businesses. Job creation cannot occur without them.

This country was founded on the principle that a new economy must be formed—one in which only the efforts and responsibilities undertaken by individuals would determine their futures. This freedom of self-determination spawned an extraordinary cultural work ethic: the mindset of an entrepreneur is what makes the difference. What is most interesting about the American work ethic is that it is most threatened when we become too comfortable. Our economic security is best served by economic discomfort. This discomfort—and it may be intellectual discomfort—is the source of all entrepreneurial activity.[4] "Creative destruction" describes the way in which capitalistic economic development arises out of the destruction of some prior economic order. (This term arose in the 1950s and is most identified with the Austrian-American economist Joseph Schumpeter.)

So where did we go wrong, and how did our country get into such a deep hole that has impacted our middle class? It started in the 1950s and '60s, when our economy was experiencing amazing growth in the post-WW II era. Our government, corporations, and unions (sometimes referred to as the "iron triangle") created the

---

[4] Schramm, *Entrepreneurial Imperative*, 11–12

environment for *bureaucratic capitalism*. These institutions worked together to provide steady growth, low inflation, and job security for all Americans. They gave rise to the role of the manager in organizational structure—the person in charge of keeping the order created by the bureaucracy. When the Cold War began to take shape, the federal government grew to "protect" America's interests, and Eisenhower's worries about the military-industrial complex materialized.

Keynesian economic policies that encouraged government spending (i.e., more debt) appeared to be the perfect tool to create the Great Society for our middle class. Bureaucratic capitalism attempted to maneuver several economic assumptions and various elements in the belief that economic growth should be predictable, that government regulations should favor consolidation of economic activity in large corporations, and that employee welfare was best protected by unionism. These capitalists believed that a stable equilibrium would be optimized for all parties involved. As a result, innovation and technological programs became systematized, and the middle class was convinced that its financial stability required the maintenance of the iron triangle.[5]

Bureaucratic capitalism has come to define the mindset of middle-class Americans through the iron triangle's concept of the economic "safety net." And what was the main focus of the safety net? A *comfortable retirement* for the entire middle class and the hardworking, blue-collar Americans who got us through WW II and into a new era of prosperity. Unfortunately, in 2014, we know that this fairy tale does not end happily for millions of Americans who believed in the story.

Retirement

Since the mid-1940s, three resources have made up the iron triangle's "three-legged stool" of financial security: company pension benefits, Social Security benefits, and personal savings. Ladies and gentlemen, the three-legged stool is broken.

You may ask where we depend on government when planning for retirement. Everyone knows that in post-WW II America, the ideal lifestyle for a man was to get a job with a good company, work there for thirty years, and collect a solid pension. Add in Social Security benefits and a little savings, and most people were content in retirement. Why? Their lifestyles were simple, they needed less money in retirement

---

[5] Schramm, *Entrepreneurial Imperative*, 11–12

because the cost of living was lower, and their houses were paid off. They had no debt and lived within their means.

The "risk" of retirement—longevity—was on the corporation and the government. The average American didn't need the stock market because CDs paid well, inflation wasn't a big deal, and taxes were reasonable. *So what changed?*

As debt and consumerism drove the economy's expansion in the 1980s and '90s, Americans formed bad habits: Corporations traded defined benefit plans (pensions) for defined contribution plans (401ks). Social Security had fewer workers paying into it and more recipients being paid out to. It became unsustainable. Personal savings rates plummeted to negative numbers in the 2000s, and people relied more heavily on the stock market to achieve their goals (i.e., make up for lost time). Investors were never educated on the risks of the market, and tax-deferred retirement accounts became ticking tax time bombs.

Now all of the risks squarely sit on the shoulders of the American taxpayer. Think about these sobering statistics:

Only 58 percent of Americans are actually saving for retirement:
- Roughly 35 percent of Americans have at least twenty-five thousand dollars saved.
- Just over 17 percent of Americans have less than one thousand dollars saved.[6]

This means that barely 6 percent of Americans have saved more than twenty-five thousand dollars for retirement. Americans from ages fifty-five to sixty-four have a median net worth of $180,000, which means that many of them appear to be financially unprepared for the retirement they want or expect. The definition of retirement continues to change because of the economic climate one retires in and the shifting social and corporate benefits offered to retirees. Relying on the government and a corporation to provide you retirement "security" can be dangerous due to the changing tides of decision makers and profit motives.[7]

Even if you make it to retirement, you still need to get all the way *through* it. To accomplish that feat, you must still deal with *taxes and inflation*. Are you confident

---

[6] Morgan Housel, "The Biggest Retirement Myth Ever Told," *The Motley Fool*, May 2, 2013
[7] Housel, "Biggest Retirement Myth"

that your current financial strategies can combat these risks? According to the IRS, in 2010, there were 140 million taxpayers, and only half of all eligible Americans actually *paid income taxes.* Total income taxes paid in 2010 were $1.031 trillion, with an effective tax rate of 12.24 percent (or $8.423 trillion in total income earned).

Digging a little deeper into the numbers, you may realize something a little troubling. The top 50 percent of all taxpayers (seventy million) paid 97 percent of all taxes (or $1.003 trillion, with an effective tax rate of 13.65 percent). These top 50 percent are defined as those with an adjusted gross income (AGI) of $33,048 or higher—not exactly a rich lifestyle.

So 50 percent of Americans pay zero dollars in income taxes, and the bottom half of the 50 percent that does pay (25 percent of the population) only pays 3 percent of the taxes. This means that 97 percent of all taxes paid in 2010 were paid by the remaining 25 percent of the population!
- o The top 10 percent (with $113,799+ AGI) pay 70 percent of total taxes.
- o The top 1 percent (with $380,354+ AGI) pay 38 percent of total taxes.

Something to consider when you hear the call to "tax the rich" to solve our budget deficits: our 2010 budget deficit was $1.3 trillion. Even if taxes were *doubled* on the top 50 percent of those who pay taxes ($33,048 AGI and above), we would still be $269 billion short.[8]

Increasing taxes is not going to solve our fiscal woes but don't think for one second that our government won't stop trying to force more of the responsibility on those who have two things it wants: income and assets.

Income can be confiscated through taxes as you earn those dollars, and inflation will extract your buying power over time—slowly but surely. Assets are impacted by taxes based on type—taxable, tax deferred, or tax exempt—while inflation erodes the value of all assets as the Federal Reserve prints more dollars. Using the CPI Inflation Calculator on www.useconomy.about.com, you can find out how much buying power a 2013 dollar would have had in the past. In 1913, it would have cost you four cents to buy something that costs one dollar today. This means that since the Federal Reserve was created, the dollar has lost 96 percent of its purchasing power.

---

[8] www.IRS.gov IRS 2010 Tax Data

As long as the Federal Reserve has access to the printing press, anyone with assets is at risk. Another way to think about this problem is through the eyes of the have-nots—people who do not make a lot of money and people who don't have enough assets to retire. Unfortunately, these groups consistently vote for whomever promises them a brighter future because no matter what, taxes and inflation are not a concern to them. So if everyone's vote is worth the same and more people are falling into the *have-not* category, I ask anyone reading this book who makes a good income or has built up a solid nest egg: who do these votes really benefit? Not the people who did a good job saving money and taking care of themselves. And not even those in the unfortunate circumstance of lacking the income or assets. Why not? Because they have no control or options in this situation. They are at the mercy of *the state.* If you really want to make it *through* retirement, not just *to* it, you have to look at your financial picture in a completely different way and consider strategies that focus on *minimizing risks* against your personal economy.

What Should You Do?

You should get educated and ask a lot of questions. Don't just listen to opinions. Find out *why* people believe something. How educated is your financial advisor in all areas of money?

Don't look to the government for answers. Entitlements are a trap. Why? They rob you of your creativity and innovation—perhaps not right away but slowly over time as they lull you into a fall sense of security. Once those promises cannot be kept, all you are left with are excuses.

The state doesn't make, produce, or create anything. Focus on minimizing risk in your financial picture because you are not entitled to anything. Go out and *earn* your accomplishments. Be realistic and start focusing your efforts toward protecting your personal economy:

- Save more (or create more money to save).
- Spend less (or figure out ways to control more of your money).
- Work longer (or smarter).

Educate. Empower. Enlighten.

Chapter 2: How I See People Make Financial Decisions

For more than eighteen years, I've seen clients of all ages and from all walks of life deal with money. These are real-life issues that today's economy creates for individuals, families, and small business owners.

New Grownups: Our Twenties

I graduated as the top finance student in the class of 1996 at Saint Louis University. That honor was greeted with several questions from my classmates and family: Are you planning on getting your master's degree in business administration (MBA)? Which big corporation do you want to work for? How much is your salary going to be?

Luckily for me, I started an internship my junior year that allowed me to get a behind-the-scenes look at the financial services industry. It was in the summer of 1995 that I realized I could be in business *for myself—but not by myself*! My compensation would be based on the value I created for my clients, and there would be no limit to what I could earn or do as an entrepreneur. For me, that was the best way to enter the *real world*—with no strings attached, no limitations, and a results-based compensation model.

I did receive a small base income of two thousand dollars per month when I started working with a group of advisors. Another entrepreneur who wanted to invest in my potential paid it to me. He mentored me in the business early on, but that base pay would only last for two years—so as not to "limit my potential." I lived at home with my mom and three siblings for five years to pay down my student loans and save up to buy a starter home. It's true that I could have worked for a big company, starting at fifty to seventy-five thousand dollars a year with the options for bonuses and promotions. But I knew that I would have been overpaid initially because I would not be bringing any *real value* to the company for a few years while I was learning. Here's how I saw it: the only reason a company would overpay me from the beginning would be a plan to *underpay* me some time in the future. I knew that later on, I would have to fight for raises and convince the company of my value. I decided that that game could be played by someone else. I've been an entrepreneur since the age of twenty-one, and I wouldn't change one thing about that decision.

Today, very few people go to school with an inner drive focused toward entrepreneurial opportunities. College degrees steer your learning toward getting a job, not building a life. An MBA is better for corporate America than it is for your advancement in society. How many people learn in school the skills of personal finance or the proper habits of saving money? Hardly anyone. Who taught you how to manage your cash flow, operate within a budget, find a place to live, or make big-ticket purchases (whether for personal, family, or business use)? Not the educational institutions to which you paid thousands of dollars (if not hundreds of thousands of dollars) to attend.

This leads young adults to start out their lives with more challenges than opportunities (assuming they have moved out of the parental home after graduation). Student loan debts are much higher now because the cost of education has increased dramatically. Who benefits from the higher debt? Not the student. Schools promise that a degree will be your ticket to success, but the skill sets learned in college don't prepare people for real-world experiences anymore. To be successful today requires more entrepreneurial initiative. It's hard to find a job that pays enough to cover repaying debts, starting a modest lifestyle, and saving all at once. Delayed gratification is not valued by our youth anymore; consumerism has overcome the benefits of being thrifty, thanks to the got-to-have-it-now mindset our media supports. Even if you find a job, you will most likely delay big-ticket life events (new car, first down payment, marriage, kids) because you cannot earn enough to build up a nest egg.

Life in Our Thirties and Forties

Entering my thirties brought more responsibility and the opportunity to create a full life. I married, and we had two beautiful children. We settled into a great neighborhood with a strong sense of community, which was *very* important to my wife. Our family values took priority; we raised our kids with an emphasis on discipline, education, and respect for others. Fortunately, my success in business allowed my wife the choice to stay home and oversee our household and the kids' daily schedules.

Money never became an issue of discontent for us simply because my wife and I built our relationship on a foundation of open communication and trust. Because of this openness, we've never experienced a marital rift over money in our fifteen years of dating and marriage. The sacrifices that we made early in our relationship have allowed us to splurge every now and then to enjoy the great life we've built together. Of course, it helps that both of us have a saver mentality and that I am fluent in the language of money, but it's still hard work to stay ahead in today's economy.

I have a simple motto: *It's only money. You can always make more.* I have confidence in my entrepreneurial abilities and understand that money is just a tool to assist in accomplishing our purposes in life. The *stuff* we buy won't make us happy or give us fulfillment. Maybe you don't see things the same way I do. But the conversations I have with my peers tell a different story.

As people in this life stage are the peers I interact with on a daily basis, I am witnessing a counterculture movement in this age group. Their lack of trust in the markets, the economy, and the government is causing them to rethink how they save and utilize their wealth.

Assuming you've created good habits of saving money, now you face difficult decisions for *using* it:

Do you buy a home to raise a family in? Have children? How many? How many children you have and how far apart they are have major impacts on your personal economy. Will you be a two-income family? You'll need daycare options until all children are in kindergarten. No matter your arrangements, the emotional and social growth of your child(ren) and being involved in their daily lives are a priority.

The economic impact of children on your personal economy is tremendous. Will you sacrifice your lifestyle so one spouse can afford to stay home? Will that decision strengthen your marriage? Does the spouse who stays at home *lose his or her identity*—or, maybe even worse, financial independence? One of the major reasons for divorce is money—or lack of it. And what type of security does the working spouse have in his or her job? Are there health benefits for the family? Where are you on the corporate ladder? Is your job in jeopardy because of your industry, corporate culture, or your skill set?

The myth of the risk/reward paradigm says when you are young, you can afford to take more risks (invest more in stocks) because you're assuming you have the time to make up for mistakes. This method assumes your biggest returns come from a buy-and-hold approach.

The reality, though, is that time is in finite quantity, and no one knows how much time he or she is granted, so protecting against loss is more valuable. The world economy and society don't always perform in concert with your timetable. Without good savings habits, you could be at the mercy of the markets.

And remember that you need to save money toward several goals simultaneously:
- Retirement
- Reducing debt
- Children's education
- Emergency fund
- Home improvements
- New automobiles
- Vacations

Those who are thrifty (frugal, cheap) sacrifice their levels of current lifestyle to ensure a *safer* personal economy. Those who are more consumer-driven may enjoy their lifestyles more in the moment, but if adequate savings habits aren't created, this situation poses real problems as they get closer to retirement. And this is most Americans. (These people would benefit more from the messages of Dave Ramsey or Suze Orman if they become reformed consumers who want to become real savers.)

As you can see in the chart below, the American personal savings rate has not been above 10 percent for thirty years.

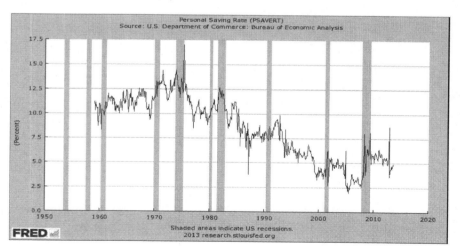

There is no magic formula to investing that can cure the ills of consumerism. It does not matter how well your investments perform if you are not contributing enough to them to grow your money over time.

Life in Our Fifties and Sixties

Since building a diverse wealth management firm, I have been fortunate to assist hundreds of clients in their fifties and sixties. Whether they were already retired or closing in on that goal, one thing was abundantly clear: the path that each client took to get to this point in financial life was based on a series of money-related decisions that will continue to impact the rest of their lives.

I'll understand if you think my words are a bit extreme, but in today's economy, you cannot just focus on getting *to* retirement. That's not the *finish line*—that's your *starting line* for the second half of your adult life!

If you have reached this period in your life financially unscathed, it means you probably experienced a good balance between work and family. After the kids were old enough for elementary school, the other spouse may have gone back to work, or your childcare expenses decreased, causing you to save more. You reduced your debt to just the home mortgage, and you're contemplating paying it off before retirement. Your job(s) have allowed you to save for retirement using specific tools (401ks and/or IRAs).

Building your nest egg most likely involved participation in the stock market or individual equities over the last twenty to thirty years. That asset class (US equities) provided you with solid appreciation and sizeable account balances. If you were a bit more conservative and complemented your equities with fixed-income assets (usually corporate or treasury bonds), you would also be in a very good position. This is because interest rates have trended downward since the early 1980s, so the value of bonds went up and provided stability to many portfolios while also generating performance that matched that of equities over time.

Unfortunately, the majority of Americans have not prepared for retirement, and they are not properly educated to figure out this dilemma on their own (as studies have shown). This lack of financial preparedness has brought about several trends impacting our current economy:

- Record consumer debt
  - Non-revolving consumer credit outstanding: $2.164 trillion as of July 2013
  - Motor vehicle loans: $839.8 billion as of mid-2013
  - Student loans: $1.178 trillion as of mid-2013[9]
- Millions of home foreclosures in the aftermath of the 2007–2008 Great Recession
- Job losses of epic proportion not seen since the 1930s
- Ever-increasing government debt to support our entitlement programs (Social Security, Medicare, and Medicaid)

These concerns are making life for all Americans more difficult, but for those who are already retired or plan on retiring in the next few years, the uncertainty is unprecedented for their generation.

Getting to Your Seventies, Eighties, and Nineties

When my grandfather Arthur retired in the early 1990s, his daily life epitomized the average American's of his time. He had served his country as a marine in WW II and then went straight to college on the GI Bill. Once out of school, Art married Marcella (everyone called her Mots), and they raised six children in the same fifteen-hundred-square-foot home they lived in for almost fifty years. Art got a job at Fabick Tractor and worked there for thirty years, serving as treasurer in his last role. Mots never worked outside of the home, but she definitely had her hands full raising six kids, putting them through private high school, and keeping them all out of trouble. Art relied on the classic "three-legged stool" to get ready for retirement—a company pension, Social Security benefits, and personal savings.

Because Art was a diligent saver and squirreled away a little bit each month, eventually retirement was possible. In his early sixties, he began his simple retirement life. Not much changed. Their budget was pretty comfortable. The mortgage had been paid off early, and the monthly income from his pension and their Social Security checks covered their regular bills with ease. They built up about $200,000 in qualified assets (in a 401k/IRA), roughly fifty thousand dollars in bank certificates of deposit, and around fifty thousand dollars in a cash-value whole life insurance contract. The couple's personal savings would be used for any

[9] "Consumer Debt 2013 Figures," http://www.federalreserve.gov/releases/g19/revisions/

financial emergencies or big-ticket items. Art had good health insurance benefits from Fabick Tractor, and Medicare took over when he turned sixty-five. He and Mots enjoyed a very peaceful retirement for more than twenty years. Art and Mots died within twelve months of each other with very few health concerns.

I say their retirement was peaceful in part because they did not have very high expectations for what their "golden years" were supposed to look like. Their life before retirement was simple and mostly uneventful, and life *after* retirement was much the same. Outside of playing a little more golf and enjoying their daily 3:00 pm cocktail (a Manhattan), they were content just spending time with their friends and family in Saint Louis. An occasional road trip to a marines' reunion would be the bulk of their travel, and they rarely flew anywhere (it was too expensive in Art's eyes).

So why am I telling you all this? Because the average American does not experience a simple retirement anymore. The act of getting *to* retirement has become more difficult, as has getting *through* retirement. The good—and bad—news is that people are living much longer. It is very probable that a number of Americans could live as many years in retirement as they did working in their jobs, careers, or businesses.

Anyone who is retired in their seventies, eighties, or nineties has a potential myriad of questions and concerns. If this is you, let me ask:

- o Does the volatility of the markets and our economy make you feel anxious?
- o Can you see the threat of inflation impacting your future?
- o Are you concerned about taxes damaging your nest egg?
- o Do you wonder if you will run out of money in retirement?
- o What will the cost of your health care be over the next ten to twenty years?
- o If your kids need financial help, is it wise for you to provide assistance?
- o Can you afford the appropriate care if you (or your spouse) get sick?
  - ▪ Will your funds cover in-home care? A nursing home?
  - ▪ Will you be cared for by a loved one or a health professional?
  - ▪ Will you have to spend down assets? Or do you have long-term care coverage?

When you get to the end of your life and you're asking yourself these tough questions, you may come to the conclusion, "This is not what I thought my golden years would be like."

So what can be done to protect your personal economy? Let's face it—the three-legged stool of retirement (the company pension, Social Security benefits, ample personal savings) is barely a memory. The idea of retirement has been manufactured to get the masses to conform. How many successful entrepreneurs do you see retired versus running their enterprises into their seventies, eighties, and nineties? Why would you ever stop doing something that you are passionate about, very good at, and highly compensated for?

The focus of life is completely off base in our country today. Happiness should come from our actions and experiences, not getting to an arbitrary finish line defined as a certain age. Thinking outside the typical mindset is extremely valuable when deciding on how to save and utilize your money over your lifetime. The more control you retain over your wealth, the easier it is to make decisions in your best interest. Do you really think that the financial institutions (banks, brokerage firms, and insurance companies) can make you rich if you save through or invest in their financial vehicles? Without true good habits, most people's financial futures are very uncertain. It is when you match the *purpose of your money* with the appropriate financial vehicles that you can actually *protect your personal economy.*

Educate. Empower. Enlighten.

Chapter 3: Your Resources—Time, Talent, and Capital

What are the building blocks to an entrepreneur's or a successful investor's decision-making process? Let's start with the resources that every human being has:

Time

Everyone has a finite amount of time. It is the scarcest resource and the one that entrepreneurs and successful investors should protect the most. For this, delegation is key. You must also surround yourself with like-minded people who not only value your time but also bring other resources to the table (their own time, talent, and/or capital) to achieve success in any of your endeavors.

The value of time as a resource is something an entrepreneur thinks about constantly. Every minute of every day is an opportunity to positively impact the life of a client, staff member, or colleague. But in today's world, protecting your time is also essential to achieving a simplified financial life. Just think about all the ways your time is "attacked" by the world around us. The Internet puts so much information at our fingertips, which can boost efficiency or be a danger. It's easy to lose track of time surfing the web or clicking on interesting links, veering off your intended course of action. In addition,

email allows us to accomplish much more in less time with nearly instant communication. Yet it can cause a lot of people to never stop working. When efficiency puts you out of balance in other areas of your life, you quickly lose sight of the big picture.

Furthermore, our cell phones are now portable offices and central nervous systems for time management. We can handle just about anything from cell phones should we dare to embrace the technologies. All of these technological advancements were designed to make our lives better, right? But do they give us more free time to spend with our families, relax, and just enjoy life more? Usually not. Instead, the average person allows other influences to control his or her time. You may be given more responsibility at work when you're efficient and effective, but does your income increase? You may take care of a lot of tasks online quickly (pay bills, shop, even do your taxes), but you also lose something: customer service. There's no human interaction anymore. People spend so much more time with their smartphones, iPads, and the latest and greatest tech toy that they forget how to communicate with each other.

A lack of communication (or unintended miscommunication) can actually waste much more time and frustrate all parties involved. Delivering information clearly and concisely is at the core of proper time management. Entrepreneurs who do this well accomplish more in less time. This causes other people to marvel at their productivity and results. Doing what you do best and delegating everything else to competent people is a practice that all people should master: you are essentially trading your capital for someone else's talent in order to free up your time. And the more time you have to focus on your own talent, the more capital you can create.

Once you gravitate to this paradigm and commit to the process, the benefits to your life are amazing. Your time is precious. There is a finite amount of it, yet we never know how much. So why waste time doing things that you are not good at? Think of all the people you interact with every day who would benefit greatly if your time were optimized: more time to go to your kids' games or school functions, a date night with your spouse every week instead of once a month, time to tune up your golf game, or spend time catching up with your friends. This is what life is all about, not material possessions or accumulating money in your investment accounts but rather *using* your resources to enhance your life experiences.

Controlling your time involves saying yes to certain things that add value and no to everything else. When it comes to your financial picture, you need to implement strategies that simplify your financial life and work with a firm that proactively communicates with you. Why? Because you will work too hard to create wealth over your lifetime. You need a firm to help you protect your personal economy so that you never have to waste a moment making up for lost time or lost capital; a firm that has the talent to minimize your risk and protect the purpose of your money can be trusted with the role of assisting you in all areas of money. That firm should understand not only that time is money but also show you how to utilize that time wisely.

Talent

Your talent is your habits, skills, and unique abilities. Understanding which talents you possess allows you to add value in all areas of your life and other people's lives. Knowing your talent gives you the ability to create capital.

Wouldn't your life be so much simpler if you could wake up every morning and focus on what you do best? When it comes to your job, career, or business enterprise, determining how you can add value in your daily routine is essential. When you work for someone else, the focus is normally on your quota, a sales goal, or impressing your manager so you can earn a bonus or a promotion. Now those special employees who can take care of their customers while appeasing upper management seem to do very well in corporate America. These talents usually lead them to receive more responsibility, job security, and company perks—at least until their company's business model changes, or the economy causes it to change its focus from customers to self-preservation.

Operating your own business is a completely different animal altogether. A lot of people perceive self-employed people as more independent and driven to do things "their way," with an ego represented by the title "president," "CEO," or "founder" after their names. While in some cases this could be an accurate depiction, a true entrepreneur is someone who wants to educate others with a vision for adding value in some area of life that brings enjoyment to clients. Entrepreneurs have a gift for surrounding themselves with other talented people and causing their collective efforts to produce results they couldn't individually.

Dan Sullivan of Strategic Coach would call this an entrepreneur's "unique ability." I have studied Dan's teachings for over fifteen years. His book, *Focusing Your Unique Ability*, outlines how you can pinpoint unique abilities. Dan explains that your own unique ability is effortless because you love to do it. It happens naturally in your daily routine. People with unique abilities need to be committed to their futures through continual learning, improving, and growing so they can create new value in the world.[10] Dan believes in a law of human existence: every human being has his or her own private experience of life. Unfortunately, the majority of us fail to manifest our uniqueness because we do not understand this principle: that your unique ability only emerges in the world through delegation. Uniqueness is a result of time and focus. For your uniqueness to emerge or become external and powerful, you must delegate to superb support persons all activities except those that call for your unique ability.[11] This process of delegation could take several years, but it is in your best interest to do it because you'll need all the time available to focus on your unique ability.

---

[10] Dan Sullivan, *Focusing Your Unique Ability*, booklet and audiotape, Toronto, Canada: The Strategic Coach Inc., 1996, 3
[11] Sullivan, *Unique Ability*, 17

Dan goes on to teach that studies of great performers in all fields support a general rule that it takes about ten thousand hours (roughly ten years) of repetition, experimentation, innovation, and formalization before a unique ability translates into genius-like activity. Making sure that your financial advisor's unique ability is protecting your personal economy should be a top priority for you.

The science of neuro-linguistic programming teaches that the purpose of modeling talent in business is to reproduce excellence. Chapter 7 discusses NLP in more depth so you can see its power for making decisions about your financial picture.

Once you determine what your two or three unique abilities or talents are in the context of business then your next step is to surround yourself with capable people. The most successful entrepreneurs find people whose unique abilities complement their talents so that delegation can occur at a high level. When someone is comfortable delegating away everything but what he or she does best, all of a sudden he or she has more time to generate additional capital.

Talent is a special human trait that needs to be nurtured and supported. Constant education that enhances someone's growth keeps talents progressing. Using your talents keeps you sharp and effective. Seeing results causes confidence to build, and one can believe that he or she is truly unique and making a difference in daily life. Without delegation and daily support, the focus on your unique abilities is negatively affected. Complexity and troubleshooting quickly sap the energy of even the savviest entrepreneur.

Life is changing at a rapid pace, so when it comes to your financial picture, surrounding yourself with a team of professionals who have expertise in all areas of money is essential. If you have access to the best minds, you're able to control your time and capital while increasing your effectiveness at a much higher level.

Capital

With the proper use of your time and a focus on your talent adding value to your career, creating capital should be the result for many. But acquiring capital doesn't always occur in an ideal timeframe. If you need capital before you create it, what are your options?

Getting access to capital is difficult in today's economic environment. You must either accumulate capital (which takes time) or borrow another person's (e.g., a family member's) or a financial institution's (e.g., a bank's) capital and manage the opportunity costs (e.g., the terms of the loan). Once you accumulate enough capital, you have control over how you allocate that resource. This is an area where entrepreneurs set themselves apart from other people.

So how do you utilize capital to create more time, talent, and capital? Let's start with turning capital into more capital. Most people refer to this process as investing. Actually, investing can be defined as "to commit money or capital in order to gain a financial return" (see www.freedictionary.com). The key word in this definition is *commit*. When you commit to something, you are accepting the risks associated with that decision. There is no certainty that your investment will produce a return or that your return will be in line with your expectations. This is why educated investors commit all their resources (time, talent, and capital) to an investment. Taking the time to perform due diligence on the appropriateness of an investment causes the investor to determine how much risk applies to the opportunity.

It doesn't matter which type of asset you are considering investing in (i.e., securities like stocks or bonds, real estate, starting a business, or a financial product purchased from an institution); minimizing risk is a true talent we should all aspire to. Reducing risk helps investors to keep more of what they make. The more capital you can retain, the better off you will be in the long run. Many entrepreneurs say they have a passion for investing. Most people misinterpret this as a love for making money. Instead, what really happens is that entrepreneurs receive enjoyment from creating more control and freedom over their time and the potential to improve their talents through positive real-life experiences.

Some would call this type of feeling "wisdom" or "a knack" for something. But when you can see a person's true talent in action, it can be an epiphany. It's a gift, and gifts are meant to be shared. Most people have a hard time understanding that their time, talent, or capital has subjective limitations. How much of these resources do you need and want so that you can enjoy your life? That question has gone unanswered for millions of Americans. They find themselves paralyzed by their limiting beliefs.

Educate. Empower. Enlighten.

Chapter 4: Understanding Your Personal Economy

Understanding the uniqueness of your personal economy is essential. There are so many elements working against individuals, families, and small business owners that sometimes working to get ahead appears futile. Why do I make this depressing-sounding comment? Because this is the exact feeling many clients have communicated directly to me as we sit down and discuss their financial pictures. Regardless of our clients' ages, occupations, incomes, or current net worth, they are all concerned about financial security or just being able to take care of their families.

If you earn enough income to pay taxes or if you've accumulated at least twenty-five thousand dollars of investable assets, you can consider yourself in select company. Why? Because only 53 percent of Americans actually pay taxes (based on 2010 figures), and only 35 percent of Americans can say they have twenty-five thousand dollars or more in savings.[12] If you think these figures are disturbing then you and I are on the same page. (If you are asking "How is that possible?" then reread the first two chapters of this book.)

Our society has been heading toward this financial abyss ever since the 1960s thanks to "The Great Society" movement and the push toward a consumption-based economy. Once the middle class started believing that the federal government, corporations, and unions were going to take care of its future needs, millions of Americans began to prioritize spending over saving. After all, our economy relies on the individual consumer to create roughly two-thirds of the country's gross domestic product (GDP). In addition, once Keynesian economics began convincing world leaders that the best way to combat a recession was for the government to pick up the slack when consumers stopped spending, budget deficits increased, and government debt rose. It is currently at $17 trillion, as the graph below illustrates.

---

[12] Housel, "Biggest Retirement Myth"

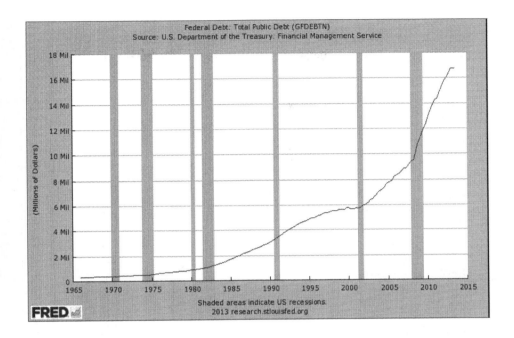

Federal Debt: Total Public Debt (GFDEBTN)
Source: U.S. Department of the Treasury: Financial Management Service

Shaded areas indicate US recessions.
2013 research.stlouisfed.org

FRED

What do you make of an entity that relies on borrowing to make up 40 percent of its annual budget? Could a family survive very long if its annual expenses were $100,000, but it had only sixty thousand dollars in income and put the other forty thousand dollars on credit cards? Absolutely not! But that is what the US government did at its peak deficit in 2010; it issued new debt to cover 40 percent of the spending from the budget.

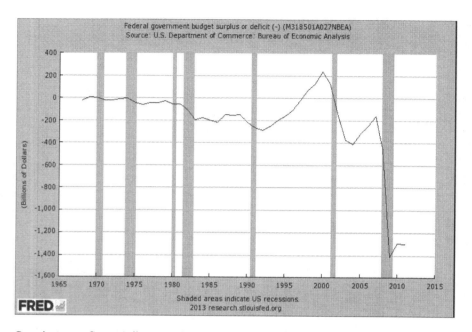

Federal government budget surplus or deficit (-) (M318501A027NBEA)
Source: U.S. Department of Commerce: Bureau of Economic Analysis

Shaded areas indicate US recessions
2013 research.stlouisfed.org

So what can financially sound individuals, families, and small business owners do to manage their *needs* while achieving their *wants* yet escape the vicious cycle of consumerism, debt burden, and entitlement traps? To get started on the journey toward protecting your personal economy, first be sure you can cover your month-to-month expenses. These are usually your financial needs. Paying the bills every month is not very exciting, but if you don't, things can be turned off or taken away. The longer your list of expenses, the higher the chance that money is flowing *out of your control* and into the control of financial institutions, lenders, credit card companies, and federal and local governments. You need to create good saving and spending habits, which can begin simply with a process to set aside a certain percentage of your income every month *first*—no matter what. Just think: if you can save 20 percent of your income automatically and use 80 percent for month-to-month expenses (needs), you create a pool of money you can use for your financial wants. Many people think this is impossible, but that is because they have a misperception that money saved should not be used. That is just false! But to make this scenario a reality, you must first comprehend the difference between your needs and wants.

We all look forward to the day when we have saved enough money to make big-ticket purchases, such as:

- A new car
- Home improvements
- Travel and vacations
- Educational expenses
- "Bucket list" items

How fantastic would it be to pay *cash* for all of these things? This can be your reality if you stick to the basics and use your money properly while it works for you. As you hit your stride, you'll save not only for big-ticket items but for longer-term goals, such as a comfortable retirement, financial security against health concerns, and protecting against economic changes that can derail even the most diligent savers. Once you understand how this is possible, financial freedom will be right around the corner. But it is important to realize that minimizing risk is vital to your journey.

Accumulation versus Utilization

If everyone had common sense for saving and investing, life would be a lot easier for all of us. It's not realistic, though, because the average American's relationship with money is built on misperceptions and myths more than it is on the fundamentals and strategies of finance. The benefits of understanding finance come over the course of time: compound interest adds growth to your principal, increasing your overall wealth. Most people implement a *buy-and-hold* approach to make money on their money, and they use *dollar-cost averaging* when buying investments to help minimize the impact of the highs and lows of market volatility.

The assumption made by the general public is that as long as you stay the course, you will reach your final destination. What we need to realize is that life doesn't happen in a straight line, and most people's financial picture is not a marathon—we don't simply wait to access our money at the finish line. Instead, financial life is more like a series of sprints or a relay race. You do everything you can to get to your next finish line, rest a little, and then get back into the starting block. But rarely do we change mindsets according to each finish line for which we need to accumulate money. So the "buy-and-hold" approach only addresses a portion of our financial responsibilities, and few financial professionals go beyond the basics of accumulation.

Most people view wealth in terms of a single number and that number is simple to determine using various online calculators. Just plug in your age, income, savings percentage, retirement age, and length of retirement, and out comes that magic number. *If only life were that simple.* A lot of variables come into play over your lifetime as you accumulate money, and the conventional wisdom has always been that long-term investors have fundamentals on their side. This mindset has been bolstered over the last thirty years as people have mainly used traditional asset classes of stocks, bonds, and cash (whatever the financial vehicle they lie behind) to hold their investments.

In fact, over the thirty years between 1981 and 2011, long-term US government bonds actually outperformed stocks measured by the S&P 500 Index 11.5 percent to 10.8 percent. This was the first thirty-year period since 1861 in which bonds outperformed stocks. A balanced portfolio of 50 percent stocks, 40 percent bonds, and 10 percent cash performed tremendously for many retirees who accumulated money in the 1980s, 1990s, and 2000s. The steady decline in interest rates over the past thirty years has meant that conservative investors received both steady income *and* appreciation from their fixed-income holdings.[13]

---

[13] "Bonds Outperform Stocks Over Past 30 Years," http://wallstcheatsheet.com/stocks/bonds-outperform-stocks-over-past-30-years.html

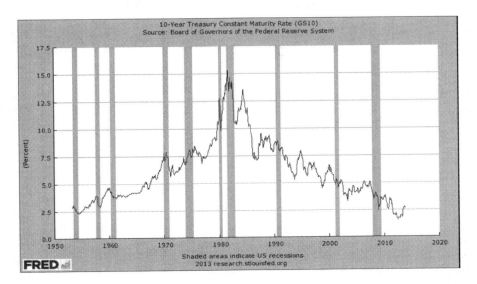

10-Year Treasury Constant Maturity Rate (GS10)
Source: Board of Governors of the Federal Reserve System

Shaded areas indicate US recessions
2013 research.stlouisfed.org

FRED

So why can't current retirees (and those close to retirement) rely on this kind of performance over the next thirty years? Current interest rates are at historical lows, so they are more likely to rise instead. As they do, bond principal will suffer. Portfolio volatilities used to be limited when they held a balance of stocks, bonds, and cash. But in today's economy, increasing interest rates can increase volatility with *both* stock and bond holdings. Compound that concern with the record amount of money in cash positions that earns Americans hardly any interest. The next two graphs illustrate these points.

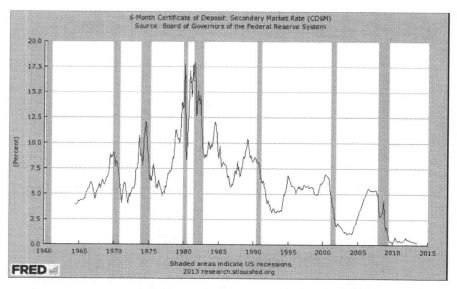

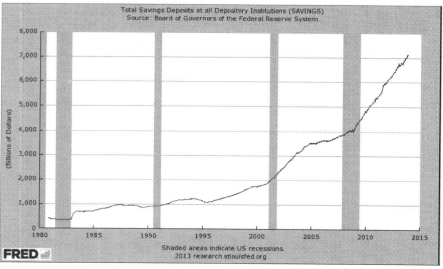

If cash pays you nothing, and bonds have increased exposure to risk as interest rates increase, the only other *traditional* asset class to use is stocks. Yet an entire generation of investors has been rattled by dismal stock performances since 2000 due to double-digit losses in four of those years.

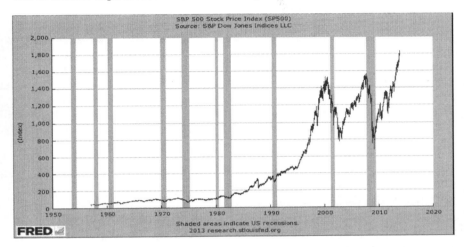

Granted, the stock market achieved all-time highs as 2013 closed, but there is a distinct distrust in the stock market's future due to the economic uncertainty that lies ahead. So what does this tell us? It tells us that we should consider changing not only which types of assets we invest in but also their purpose. Why save money just to let it sit in an account forever? The purpose of saving money is *to use it*!

Those infatuated with accumulating money rarely consider the utilization of those dollars simultaneously. Since no one has the luxury of making financial decisions in a vacuum, we must take into account the present situation and strategies for the future. The past is only relevant for learning from experience—not for repeating. People are infatuated with rates of return but do not understand *how* certain assets generate growth from income and/or appreciation. On top of that, very few advisors explain to their clients the different types of returns your personal economy can benefit from.

Internal, External, and Eternal Rates of Return

Habits are the key to financial success. It doesn't matter how much money you make, save, inherit, or receive if you don't have solid habits: saving first and spending less than you have. Otherwise, your financial picture could be in jeopardy.

For many of you, it would be prudent to make your assets work for you by putting your money in asset classes that create growth through income first. Also understand that you have several ways to create returns.

Internal return is what your asset generates through its performance (both income and appreciation over time). In most cases, this is calculated as the return on investment (ROI). Most retail, market-driven vehicles (stocks, mutual funds, and exchange-traded funds [ETFs]) use this return to measure their performance. They provide reports that show average returns over a specific period (one year, three years, five years, ten years, and since inception). Your internal return is specific to your timeline of action and cannot be truly determined until after you've completed your investment horizon.

And always remember that *past performance is no indication of future results*. You hear this all the time, but most financial advisors disregard this principle when making investment recommendations. But internal return is normally out of your control because you have no way to know how much appreciation you'll earn from the market. Utilizing asset classes that generate growth through income first can assist you in creating a more stable internal return.

External return is rarely considered, but entrepreneurs and institutions take advantage of this factor all the time. Think of it as *return on cash flow*. When you properly utilize your money and leverage your internal return by getting more of your money to flow into your control, the results are magnified. You can do this by minimizing the opportunity costs that impact your daily life, such as:

- Interest costs from banks, credit cards, and mortgage companies
- Lack of control of your principal as you pay down debt
- Restricting the use of your money to one goal only
- Being held hostage by income taxes when you want to access your money

External return is *subjective* because everyone's financial picture is different. When an entrepreneur buys a business, its initial internal return is based on its cash flow and business valuation. Now the buyer can add an external return by reducing expenses through operational synergies, improved employee morale with a better work environment, and visionary leadership. Add in some management expertise that can improve the trajectory of the company's future, and all of a sudden the value of the business could improve five to ten times.

You can accomplish something similar by operating your personal economy the same way. You first need to realize that *cash flow is everything*. Managing your budget to keep spending on a realistic path while simultaneously building savings is extremely difficult. This is why most small businesses fail within their first three to five years. But if you can follow sound financial principles within your own financial home, generations of your family can enjoy the benefits.

Next, you should implement financial strategies that get money flowing into your control without completely depleting your savings or access to capital. Paying off credit card debt, student loans, and your home is a very beneficial financial strategy, but if you leave yourself with zero savings to accomplish these goals, you could wind up vulnerable should an unexpected event occur with your job, health, or family that affects you financially. So figuring out ways to have your money work for you while you use it is critical, and we'll discuss those techniques later in this book.

Let's look at a few examples just to get a sense of this concept:

Example 1: Paying Off Debt

Let's say you have fifty thousand dollars ($50,000) of household income and twenty thousand dollars ($20,000) in the bank making virtually nothing (less than 1 percent interest). Your monthly debt payments are:

- $500 to low-interest credit cards with a $10,000 balance at 5 percent interest
- A $250 student loan payment (also a $10,000 balance at 5 percent)

This $750 per month adds up to nine thousand dollars ($9,000) per year or 18 percent of your income.

Should you pay off these debts with the $20,000 of cash you have in the bank? Conventional wisdom says that doing so will save you the 5 percent interest paid to the credit card and student loan companies (this is the internal rate of return).

But what is your increased cash flow when you pay off the debts? It's the amount you no longer pay out per year: $9,000 or 18 percent. This is the sum of the 5 percent internal rate of return plus the 13 percent external return from the principal.

However, this comes with an opportunity cost: the lack of cash for an emergency fund. In other words, liquidity is eliminated while cash flow is dramatically increased.

Another option is to pay off the credit card first and then pay off the student loan in the next year or so. You pay off the credit card first because it has a higher return on cash flow for the same amount of debt ($500 per month saved is a 12-percent increase to cash flow).

Example 2: Paying Off Your Home

In this example, you have $100,000 in household income. You have a $150,000, thirty-year mortgage at 4 percent. Your required house payment is only $716 in principal and interest (we'll leave out taxes and insurance because some people build these costs into their payment, and others pay them separately). You are also very conservative and don't like debt of any kind, so you also pay $284 extra to reduce your principal faster.

You have $200,000 sitting in the bank, making less than 1 percent interest. What happens if you pay off your mortgage now with $150,000 from your savings? You'd save twelve thousand dollars ($12,000) per year in cash flow, an increase of 12 percent (9 to 10 percent external return plus 2 to 3 percent internal).

Why not 4 percent internal return (the loan rate)? Well, the loan amortization only requires $180 to $220 per month in interest; the rest is principal. So your interest saved is $2,160 to $2,640 per year or 2 to 3 percent.

What are your opportunity costs? You have less liquidity—you cannot access your $150,000 anymore when you put it into the house unless you sell the property or take out another mortgage (or home equity loan). In other words, the money "in" the home stops working for you—it's making a 0-percent internal return.

Many clients ask, "Doesn't the house still appreciate?" Well, we hope so. But if it does, it appreciates whether you have a mortgage on the property or not. So, no, the $150,000 mortgage payoff in this case *is not working for you*.

This is one big reason I am a proponent of certain types of alternative assets for these types of big-ticket items. If structured properly, certain assets can produce both internal and external returns *while* you use the money.

Now I am sure some readers are wondering, *Which return is more valuable to me—internal or external?* That's not the way to look at them, though. Instead, you need to look at your financial picture and see how each return impacts your personal economy. The lower your asset values, the greater impact external returns will have on your financial picture.

Example 3

You make $100,000 and have $100,000 in assets. If you save 10 percent of your income ($10,000 per year), that is an external return that *you control*. To create the same accumulation results compared to your cash flow, you would need to make a 10-percent internal return on your assets. Based on our current economy, how much risk are you willing to take to achieve that 10 percent—knowing that you could also lose money?

If you have accumulated more assets, the effectiveness of your internal return is magnified.

Example 4

You make $100,000 and have $500,000 in assets. You save the same amount as above (a 10-percent external return). But now you only need to generate a 2-percent internal return to equal your cash flow results. However, the more assets you accumulate, the bigger the risk of loss.

You still want to save 10 percent of your cash flow, but you also want your assets working for you as hard as possible without too much risk. You must find an investment strategy that minimizes risk while achieving an expected internal return. Your financial professional needs to align with it.

Let's compare strategies for accumulating $500,000.

- Saving ten thousand dollars ($10,000) per year and earning a 0-percent internal return, it would take you fifty years.
- With a 5-percent internal return, you cut that time almost in half (25.7 years).
- With an 8-percent internal return, it takes twenty-one years.
- With a 10-percent internal return, it takes nineteen years.

All of these calculations assume that you earn these internal rates every year without interruption—that's not very realistic. The more internal return you seek to create, the more important a risk minimization strategy becomes.

Most people who are successful at building first-generation wealth intend to leave legacies for multiple generations to use and carry forward. This is what I call the *Eternal return*. It is the culmination of your time, talent, and capital passed on to the next generation. It can comprise assets, the knowledge you impart to your family during your life, and the goodwill you have created for your family legacy. This type of return includes a lot of intangibles and is sometimes difficult to grasp but make no mistake—it could be the most valuable return of all. If structured properly, the wealth you've created can improve your family's personal economy five, ten, twenty, even a hundred times over because its members are now working from a more robust, solid foundation that *you* built over time.

With an uncertain economic outlook for America over the next thirty years, families that provide an eternal return to the next generations may be protecting not only their personal economies but their families' economic survival.

Past, Present, and Future Mentalities

It has been my experience that people's perceptions of rates of return, investments, and risk are very subjective. Before I can assist my clients with strategies that protect their personal economies, I need to understand from which of three general perspectives they view money-related decisions: based in the past, present, or future. Money and wealth are abstract concepts because people normally make decisions based on a finite amount of information and a subjective perspective crafted from their life experiences. There is no such thing as a right or wrong decision about money. Neuro-linguistic programming teaches this mindset and has helped me understand how different clients react very differently to virtually the same set of money-related scenarios.

The Past-Based Perspective

People with the past-based perspective believe that a lot can be learned from things that have already occurred. In fact, they believe that *history repeats itself*. They use data on what has happened before to convince themselves that certain strategies make sense because "the results speak for themselves." These folks also rely on conversations with trusted family, friends, colleagues, or advisors who have "been there, done that" and on the anecdotes about their experiences. With no real-life experiences of his or her own to draw from, the information-seeker tends to generalize from what he or she hears.

However, it is important to remember this common disclosure in the investment industry: "past performance is no indication of future results." Even though the track record of a certain investment—whether one year long, ten years long, or over its lifetime history—may look good on paper, another phrase is needed for a proper grasp on reality: "that was then; this is now."

If you get caught in a past-based mindset, it can be very difficult for you to make a decision and move forward. "Should" is a favorite word within limiting beliefs. Second-guessing and Monday-morning quarterbacking are rampant with past-based financial thinking and usually keep people from moving forward with any type of significant action.

The Present-Based Perspective

Making financial and money-related decisions can be difficult if you only use a past-based perspective. Learn from your victories and your defeats. The world economy is in a constant state of flux. Whether you realize it or not, your personal economy can be directly impacted by something that happens thousands of miles away. You need to implement strategies that provide as much flexibility and control over your money as possible without sacrificing the results you desire. Change is a constant variable in all of our lives, yet most people do everything possible to keep their financial affairs in a "status quo" position.

The key is to educate yourself. Remember our phrase from chapter 1—"knowledge is power"—and sidestep the inaction based on the fear of making the wrong decision. The crisis of confidence we see today manifests itself in several areas of the economy: housing, workforce, banking, investing, politics, and business, to name a few. What are average Americans supposed to do? Get educated. Become empowered. Experience enlightenment.

Expand your knowledge beyond *what most people do with their money.* Create certainty with a mindset that fits *your* needs and wants. You need to work with financial professionals who speak with you transparently and can help you implement customized, one-size-fits-one strategies. You need realistic expectations that assist you in using your money under an education-based advising model aimed at achieving a financial balance.

The Future-Based Perspective

If you look forward instead of back, you can deal with change and the unknown strategically. Once your financial education builds you a foundation of confidence, you can take action. This entire process often begins with good, solid questions—so you can open your mind to solutions that you may never have considered. The right financial professional or firm adds value with questions that address your needs, wants, and risks.

For you to feel successful in your financial life, managing your expectations is critical: continuous communication is essential. Ideally, trust builds between you and your financial professional. Once you get some results, assess them, make any necessary changes to stay on track, and continue moving forward. Remember, change is the one constant here.

However, don't focus your energy on the things that you *cannot* control (the government, the Federal Reserve, interest rates, stock market performance, your health, and so on) that impact your personal economy.

Instead, turn to the areas that you *do control*:

- The flow of your money
- How your savings and investments are taxed
- Determining the purpose of your money
- Identifying the major risks that threaten your personal economy

All this may seem like an overwhelming responsibility, but instead of thinking that there's no way you can do it, ask, "What would my life be like if I did take control of my financial picture?"

Educate. Empower. Enlighten.

Chapter 5: Why a Solution Matters Today More Than Ever

In 2013, I was introduced to an amazing book: Simon Sinek's *Start with the Why-How Great Leaders Inspire Everyone to Take Action*.[14] It completely changed the way I communicate my firm's vision and our purpose. Its message is so powerful because it explains the best way I've seen to communicate the why, how, and what of one's business to potential clients. Simon refers to these aspects of a business as the Golden Circle[15]:

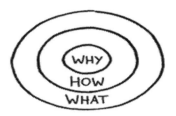

The Golden Circle

What
Every organization on the planet knows WHAT they do. These are products they sell or the services they offer.

How
Some organizations know HOW they do it. These are the things that make them special or set them apart from their competition.

Why
Very few organizations know WHY they do what they do. WHY is not about making money. That's a result. It's a purpose, cause or belief. It's the very reason your organization exists.

© 2013 Simon Sinek, Inc.

He explains very simply the power of the Golden Circle[16]

Every single organization on the planet, even our own careers, always functions on three levels. What we do, How we do it and Why we do it. When all those pieces are aligned, it gives us a filter through which to make decisions. It provides a foundation for innovation. When all three pieces are in balance, others will say, with absolute clarity and certainty, "We know who you are," "We know what you stand for." Whether they realize it or not, all great and inspiring leaders and organizations think, act and communicate just like each other...and it's the complete opposite from everyone else.

---

[14] Simon Sinek, *Start with Why: How Great Leaders Inspire Everyone to Take Action*, Portfolio Trade, 2009
[15] Downloadable Powerpoint presentation, "GC_slides_v1.4," http://www.startwithwhy.com
[16] "GC_slides_v1.4" authorization to use material provided at the time information was downloaded.

Every company or organization knows WHAT they do. These are the products we sell or the services we provide.

Some companies and organizations know HOW they do what they do. The "differentiating value proposition" or "proprietary process" or "USP," these are the things that set us apart from our competition; the things we think make us special or different from everyone else.

Very few people and organizations can clearly articulate WHY they do what they do. Why is a purpose, a cause or a belief. It provides a clear answer to Why we get out of bed in the morning, Why our company even exists and why that should matter to anyone else. Making money is NOT a Why. Revenues, profits, salaries and other monetary measurements are simply results of what we do. The Why inspires us.

We naturally communicate from the outside-in, we go from the clearest thing to the fuzziest thing. We tell people WHAT we do, we tell them HOW we're different or special and then we expect a behavior like a purchase, a vote or support. The problem is that WHAT and HOW do not inspire action. Facts and figures make rational sense, but we don't make decisions purely based on facts and figures. Starting with What is what commodities do. Starting with Why is what leaders do. Leaders inspire.

Leaders and organizations with the capacity to inspire think, act and communicate from the inside-out. They start with Why. When we communicate our purpose or cause first, we communicate in a way that drives decision-making and behavior. It literally taps the part of the brain that inspires behavior.

Sinek inspired me to focus my attention on our firm's *why* and take action by authoring a book of my own. Let me briefly explain our firm's *why* and the importance of igniting that entrepreneurial drive in all of us. The rest of the book will educate you on the tools and strategies I believe are necessary for individuals, families, and small businesses to take control of their financial pictures and protect their personal economies.

My financial firm's *why* is:

> To proactively challenge the status quo as to how Americans
> are educated about finance and money related decisions.

I believe that the "status quo" of American financial education is to rely on the
authority of:

- The government
- The Federal Reserve
- Financial institutions (banks, mutual fund companies, brokerage firms)
- The media (including the Internet)
- Conventional wisdom from "talking heads"

All of these entities want to control how you *think, communicate, and behave* in
your decisions about finance and money.

The Government

The government doesn't create anything. It does not produce, manufacture, or build
anything. Its employees are paid with *your* money (tax dollars). Any promises that
a government official makes must be delivered by someone else in the future, but
that future person may hold different views on what is in your best interest.
Growing the government is not a way to grow the economy. The government wants
you to rely on it for everything: a job, your safety, retirement savings, health care,
a stable economy. For this reason, many Americans worry about the "socialization"
of our economy.

The Federal Reserve

I consider the Federal Reserve the government's henchman: if it can't get what it
needs through *taxes*, the Fed will just print the rest. Doing that causes currency to
inflate. This means that the government effectively uses *inflation* as a tool to control
your money. Inflation is a much bigger risk to those who are not rich because they
cannot protect their incomes or assets; their resources (education, expertise, access
to teams of professionals) are limited.

The Fed says that its goal is to get unemployment to 6.5 percent while keeping
inflation below 3 percent. But the trick is in how unemployment and inflation are

calculated. If you want to learn the truth behind these figures, check out these links:

http://www.huffingtonpost.com/2013/07/19/unemployment-rate-wrong_n_3619152.html

http://www.americanthinker.com/blog/2012/03/whats_the_real_rate_of_inflation.html

The Fed creates bubbles in the economy and makes excuses when things go bad. Who ends up getting hurt? Not the rich.

Financial Institutions

Financial institutions need and want your money too. How do they get it? They charge you fees for transactions and their "expert" management. How easy is it to get your money out of these institutions when you want or need it?

Banks earn interest on money they lend out, but they either use your money (in the form of deposits) *or* they can borrow from the Federal Reserve. This mechanism is highly inflationary thanks to the fractional reserve banking system we have accepted since 1913.

Fee-based advice from brokerage firms or independent advisors is a popular method of managing assets. These firms gather assets to charge a set fee for providing you advice on how to invest and allocate your money. Where is the problem with this setup? There's nothing wrong with a "fee-for-service" model or the idea of giving you *objective* advice not tied to products or commissions. But here's the reality: advisors don't control the performance of those investments. You only make money when those accounts go up. But the advisor makes money in any market environment: up, down, or flat. So, unless you're getting value in some other area, you may end up disappointed.

The Media

Information overload is the media's main objective. It's up to you to figure out which information is useful in your situation. Most people get confused because complexity is the norm today. Every medium is used to promote the latest financial "cure"—"buy my book," "watch my show," "read my newsletter," "listen to my top three strategies," and you'll be all set, right? The media's approach is based on a herd mentality for making decisions: it doesn't allow for customization. These kinds of financial "experts" are quick to give their opinions without ever looking at *your* financial picture.

Conventional Wisdom

I get a kick out of the media's talking heads spouting their predictions every day so that all may marvel at their analysis by peering through a crystal ball . Every financial show gives you two-minute glimpses into their "experts'" opinions on a topic. Bull or bear? Inflation or deflation? Save or spend...who's right? Which scenario applies to your situation? And how do you ever know who made the right call?

I believe that when the forces are working against you, it's because it's in *their* best interests to do so. Do you ever hear something on TV or read something somewhere from one of these sources and think, *That doesn't make any sense...why would they do or say such a thing?* Instead, ask this: "Who benefits by saying this?" The answer will uncover more truth than you can possibly imagine—especially when it comes to creating, protecting, and transferring your wealth.

How Do You Define Wealth?

People throw the word "wealth" around a lot, but the definition of wealth is subjective. Its meaning in your personal economy is the one you give it! The encyclopedia's definition is "the abundance of valuable resources or material possessions." And each individual defines abundance differently. I have found the subject fascinating—yet the subject of wealth can actually be intimidating to people. For example, some people have told me that because I say I run a "wealth management" firm, they are probably not good clients for us since they are not "wealthy." Can you believe that?

So, yes, wealth means different things to different people. But it can include a lot of components; money, various assets, and material possessions are just the tip of the iceberg for the truly wealthy. I will discuss the various asset classes used by the wealthy to minimize their risks later in this book so stay tuned. Abundance is a mindset. Notice how you think, communicate, and behave around people who you believe are *truly* wealthy. It will tell you a lot.

The truth is that my wealthiest clients don't necessarily have millions of dollars. Their wealth resides in several areas of their lives that create *balance*:

- Happiness and comfort around living in the moment
- Enjoying their big-ticket items (second home, travel, hobbies)
- Good health for themselves (and their parents)
- A multigenerational family presence (parents, kids, and grandchildren with strong bonds that create powerful memories)
- Giving back to society, paying it forward (fundraising for charities and foundations)

Now, this type of balanced lifestyle can be supported by fifty thousand dollars in assets or $5 million. What *really* matters are the fundamentals of your money habits—saving more than you spend (preserving cash flow) and controlling your money's flow. You'll have the peace of mind that your personal economy is protected.

If you really focus on how your money gets used then, over time, more of your money can flow into your control. Paying interest to financial institutions (banks, mortgage companies, credit card companies) and allowing the government to imprison you with taxes and inflation are not in your best interest. Educate yourself on ways to properly structure the growth profile of your money and take control of your financial picture.

I believe that everyone has three resources for improving their lives: time, talent, and capital. Those who figure out how to leverage their *time* to improve their *talent* so that they can create *capital* are special—I call them entrepreneurs. If everyone could learn how to handle their financial pictures like successful entrepreneurs, the reliance on government and financial institutions would disappear, and more people would realize the American dream. Then the whole country could understand what real wealth looks like.

First-Generation Wealth

Understanding the definition of wealth and how to use it should be accompanied by the answer to this question: where does wealth come from?

Inherit It

Of the top one hundred entries on the 2013 Forbes 400 list of the richest people, 45 percent inherited their wealth. An entire industry caters to these billionaires with family office services that take care of their every need, wish, desire, or concern. With any amount of inheritance, the focus becomes twofold: what to do with the funds now that they are available and how to protect them so that they don't disappear. It may seem as if inheriting wealth is an easy way to acquire financial independence, but if good money habits and expert financial knowledge are not in place, the wealth could be gone before the next generation gets to see it, no matter the amount.

Make It Yourself

This is the tried-and-true method by which the average American builds financial independence—through hard work and good habits. Most people who accomplish this feat in this way do it by saving and investing their money wisely and over decades (from twenty to forty years). The stock market has played a huge role in this process over the past thirty-plus years. The main financial goal most people have is a comfortable retirement, so their focus tends to be long term in nature. With access to vehicles such as 401ks, Roth IRAs, and tax laws permitting larger tax-deferred contributions, building a nest egg for retirement has been more attainable for savers.

Unfortunately, there are big flaws in this method of wealth building: nobody has control over the performance of the stock market or the economy, plus there is the difficulty of balancing the financial needs of a family for the twenty or thirty years leading up to retirement. The continued manipulation of our currency makes the economy unstable and can produce "asset bubbles" that turn people's nest eggs into scrambled eggs in a matter of years (or even months). We witnessed this reality in 2000 through 2002 and then 2007 and 2008, when millions of Americans lost their jobs and watched their asset balances crater. Confidence in a better life deteriorated.

While people are maximizing the funding of their 401ks and accumulating tax-deferred assets because of the out-of-sight, out-of-mind simplicity of these vehicles, they struggle to balance the utilization of their money for big-ticket items (paying off debt, purchasing a vehicle, buying a home, funding their children's education, and so on). There's no clear-cut "how-to" method for families to handle these financial needs; in addition, the landscape of where to put the savings earmarked for these items has drastically changed. The benefit of setting money aside in money market accounts or bank CDs is limited these days. The interest barely covers the fees on bank accounts. Bonds used to be another safe haven for these big-ticket item funds, but with interest rates at the bottom of a thirty-year cycle, the concern over principal loss and illiquidity has increased investors' concerns about this asset class.[17]

The way that people have accumulated wealth over the past thirty years (in the traditional asset classes of stocks, bonds, and cash) no longer offers the same risk-return profile. Thus, more and more Americans worry about longevity risk: running out of money before they run out of time. Why is this a risk that people face today? It's simple—we are all living longer, and the money we save for retirement needs to not only get us *to* retirement but also *through* retirement. Couple that fact with the uncertainty in the US health care industry, and you can see that our country's future financial health is extremely fragile.

So if it is becoming difficult to *keep* the wealth we make (causing families to pass on less money to their heirs), what are the options for today's American families and future generations?

Create the Wealth

When I say "create the wealth," I mean that you should determine how to add value for others and receive compensation for your efforts. Whether you are an entrepreneur or an employee, you have the ability to control the environment you work in. Now if you've never had money then you are embarking on a mission to bring first-generation wealth to your family. If you succeed, your family's future will be filled with more possibilities and opportunities because resources will be available that did not exist before.

Habits to Create First-Generation Wealth

Manage your cash flow so that you always live below your means. This does not mean your budget is all about pinching pennies. You just need to structure your

---

[17] National Planning Corporation Disclosure - Bank CDs are FDIC insured and offer a fixed rate of return, whereas both principal and yield of investment securities do have risk and may fluctuate with changes in market conditions. In general, the bond market is volatile and fixed income securities carry interest rate risk, among others. Any fixed income security sold or redeemed prior to maturity may be subject to a substantial gain or loss.

budget so that you are always saving 15 to 20 percent of your annual income. Think of this as your "profit margin," just like a well-run company would. Depending on the type of income source you have, this method of saving will be more or less flexible.

If 100 percent of your income is from salary or wages then you should be sure to "pay yourself first." This means setting aside 15 to 20 percent of every check while the rest goes to your month-to-month expenses. Your 15- to 20-percent savings are for spending on your big-ticket Items.

If your income is made up of salary and commissions or bonuses then you have more flexibility in managing your cash flow and building your wealth. Your variable income (commissions or bonus) is directly linked to your performance, so you control that. Put 10 to 15 percent of your *salary* into a 401k, Roth IRA, or other retirement vehicle and live on the rest; put the bonus/commissions into your savings for big-ticket items.

This savings structure could be difficult for some people: their salaries might only be half of their total compensation, or 100 percent of their income could be commission-based. The key is to create good habits and flexibility in your budget. But in any business where sales income is a direct component of compensation, it's important to realize that things can change from year to year (including whether you are employed at all). Building a rainy-day fund is for making sure you have what you need every month to keep the lights on, not for keeping up with the Joneses.

If you own your own business, you will need to keep both business and personal budgets that abide by these rules. Depending on the business you are in and how successful it is, you may want to consider "investing" more of your wealth back into your business. Why?

If your business is creating 15- or 20-percent profit margins (or more), you'll be hard pressed to find any other asset class that can generate that much return. So investing more in your business has the potential to create more wealth and provide you with all the money you need to handle your personal month-to-month expenses and big-ticket items.

Here are a few key action items for protecting your personal economy:

Focus on *minimizing risk* with what you've saved.
- Your main risks are market volatility, inflation, taxes, and longevity.
- Understand how alternative asset classes can help you take control of your financial picture.

Design your cash flow system to give yourself more control.
- Balance this design with potential opportunity costs in mind.

Remember that the government wants to control your money so it can use it; its tools are taxes and inflation. Financial institutions want to control your money so they can make money on it. This normally occurs when people accumulate debt. And the financial institutions control the terms of the loan (interest rate, amortization period, and calculation of the monthly payment).

Educate. Empower. Enlighten.

Chapter 6: Think Like the Rich

Since I was fifteen years old, I have worked for and alongside many successful businesspeople, entrepreneurs, and investors. Those experiences are what led me to start a career in financial services at the young age of twenty-one. The occupations of my mentors ranged from multimillionaire CEOs to policemen, teachers, lawyers, corporate executives, and passionate small business owners. The lessons I learned about how each of them made financial and money-related decisions taught me about a disturbing reality: there *is* a huge difference between "the rich" and everyone else. But listen very closely to this: *the difference has nothing to do with money*! It has everything to do with their *access* to information, *confidence* in their own abilities, and the *resources* they utilize when taking *action*. Once I grasped these economic truths and began working with my clients as a financial advisor, I developed a laser-clear focus on bridging the gap for anyone who would listen to me.

As my knowledge in these areas increased, and I evolved my own perspective on wealth, a personal transformation took place. And my business transformed from a financial advisory practice to a wealth management firm that offered "family office"-type resources to all of our clients. These changes brought a different environment to our firm. We attracted clients who wanted to not only know more but *do* more with their finances. I felt the exact same way about my own and began looking at myself as an entrepreneur in the wealth management industry. I saw that the traditional financial strategies promoted by most financial advisors were falling short of their objectives: *to protect clients' personal economies.*

You'll soon find out how you can think like the rich. I'll give you some insight on how certain financial institutions (namely, endowments and pensions) manage their money because their entire existence revolves around *using* their monies. Sound familiar? Once you understand the basics of a rich person's mindset, I'll teach you a process and philosophy that empowers anyone with good money habits to take control of their financial pictures.

Why should this subject be important to average Americans? Because they can understand how the rich create, use, and protect their wealth. This knowledge can assist people at all economic levels because the "money secrets" of the rich are more about their habits and decision-making processes—which all people can model.

Understanding the role that a family office plays in the financial elite's daily lives is a big part of this thought process. Investopedia defines them this way:

> *Family offices are private wealth management advisory firms that serve ultra-high net worth investors. Family offices are different from traditional wealth management shops in that they offer a total outsourced solution to managing the financial and investment side of an affluent individual or family. For example, many family offices offer budgeting, insurance, charitable giving, family-owned businesses, wealth transfer and tax services.[18]*

Single-family offices gained popularity in the 1800s to manage the burgeoning fortunes of tycoons such as the Rockefellers. The offices offer many of the same services as top-tier private banks and wealth managers but are devoted to a single family. The attention can cost $1 million or more per year, industry experts say, meaning family offices make financial sense mainly for families with at least $100 million in assets. There are about five thousand such households in the United States, according to the Family Wealth Alliance, a research and consulting firm in Wheaton, Illinois, and Wealth-X, a wealth research firm based in Singapore.

In *The Family Office: Advising the Financial Elite* by Russ Alan Prince (2010), he considers the following: who are the "financial elite," and how much money does it take to be considered part of this group? Mainly individuals and families with a net worth of $20 million or more qualify as financial elite, but a separate category, the "super-rich," would have $500 million+ in net worth. Regardless of the size of their wealth, they crave privacy and confidentiality. They demand white glove service and leading-edge thinking from the professionals turned to for guidance and support.[19] There are two main types of financial elite:

Wealth preservers—on average they are more affluent, but their assets are not as liquid. They focus on maintaining their wealth.

Wealth creators—these people are not as affluent as wealth preservers, but their monies are more liquid. They want to increase their fortunes, and investing plays a crucial role in this process.

---

[18] "Definition of Family Offices," http://www.investopedia.com/terms/f/family-offices.asp
[19] Russ Alan Prince, *The Family Office: Advising the Financial Elite,* 2010, 17

The sheer number of financial elite and the aggregate wealth they control are difficult to obtain due to the privacy surrounding this amount of wealth. Figures from 2010 estimated a range of 564,000 to 1,209,000 families that controlled $63.8 to $129.1 trillion in assets. Maintaining order with this amount of wealth can be difficult, so Prince describes critical "money rules" that are essential for the financial elite as they maintain a successful "Personal Wealth Creation Program."

The financial elite must commit to what Prince calls "extreme wealth. " Many people would like to be rich but haven't committed the time or effort necessary to get there. Most people are more talk than action. "What are you NOT willing to do?" is the important question to ask oneself. Next, engaging in enlightened self-interest allows the wealthiest among us to focus on reaching their specific goals and never waver or allow themselves to be derailed by the chance for group happiness. This mindset becomes important in several business settings—especially in negotiations (quote from Bill Gates: "In business, you don't get what you deserve but only what you negotiate.").

An important element to the super-rich's wealth is they tend to have equity stakes in enterprises that, they conclude, are likely to make them wealthier. The multiplier effect of these equity stakes is what generates the significantly above-average returns you hear or read about in the news. They believe being your own boss gives you a greater chance for wealth versus working for someone else. The desire to pursue the fields and initiatives that have the highest potential for outsized returns, now and in the future, is a main force behind their entrepreneurial nature.

But the financial elite are not the only ones who can benefit from this mindset. The exceedingly wealthy assume everyone has a degree of self-interest that can be used to their advantage, and they target that nature in others when building a team around themselves. They reward that team handsomely—with cash, equity, or some other form of currency—in an effort to cultivate the loyalty and specific behaviors in their colleagues that can help them advance toward their long-term goals. This team mentality extends into the realm of networking as the financial elite connect with others for profit and results. Highly successful people think about networking as a means to an end because they maximize time and effort spent towards influence over others. They desire to maintain a small but deep network of relationships that leads not to friendship but power and influence. Those financial elite that master this trade participate in "nodal networking." This is when a person has a few very powerful, highly targeted, deep relationships with people who in turn have an array of similar relationships of their own. The super-rich are able to maximize their time and efforts as they connect for profit (first indirectly then directly) with a wide variety of people who can make them wealthier.

While the lives of the financial elite may be filled with success in many areas, that does not make them immune to failure. Utilizing failure to improve and refocus is at the core of both wealth preservers and wealth creators. They know failure is inevitable, but learning from each experience and using those lessons to get an advantage the next time around actually energize them to achieve more "the next time around." This level of perseverance is not witnessed in the average American's daily life and causes most people to "get in their own way" and not achieve the level of success desired.

The wealthiest among us know there are very few things they do well, what they want to achieve, and which role they play in generating wealth. Dan Sullivan calls this someone's unique ability. Others may describe this as being highly centered. This means sticking to your plan and not getting distracted by other opportunities or events that call for new and different skill sets. The super-rich are exceptionally capable of focusing themselves and delegating to others in a way that leaves little room for derailment or doubt. This fact is what makes family offices a valued part of the financial elite's world.

Family offices tend to be highly responsive to their clients' needs. Because of their extensive amount of resources and multiple areas of expertise, family offices can provide a holistic approach to any money-related decision. This allows them to create customized solutions that are not based on any specific products.[20]

The array of family office services mainly depends on the principals' backgrounds but certainly will include the main areas of wealth management: investment management, advanced planning, and private banking. Wealthy investors are comfortable with both traditional asset management approaches as well as alternative investment strategies (e.g., hedge funds and private equity). Due to the size of their net worth, family office clients will desire the coordination of their estate plans and asset protection strategies, especially if business interests are included in their financial affairs. Buying and selling business interests, raising capital, and working with financial institutions are several ways a family office can

---

[20] Prince, *The Family Office*, 51

add value for their clients.[21] Additional support services can be provided in nonfinancial areas as listed below:

SUPPORT SERVICES
Administrative
- Data aggregation
- Bill paying
- Tax preparation or coordination
- Acting as the day-to-day CFO

Lifestyle
- Family security
- Concierge services
- Medical concierge
- Philanthropic advisory
- Formal family education
- Managing fine art/collectibles
- Property management

The sheer scope of possibilities and combinations means that truly unique and thorny issues can be addressed in a wholly customized fashion without deviating from the basic operating structure. Customization also occurs when family offices are compensated. The various methods of fees paid (retainer, transaction based, consulting, or "success driven") can also accompany potential equity deals when a client wants a partner and is comfortable with giving up "a piece of the action." Ultimately, the compensation is based on performance and managing their clients' expectations.

Now I am sure that some readers are wondering, *How does any of this information apply to me? I will never be rich or in the financial elite.* Look, that's one of the problems that I face with clients on a daily basis. You feel that you need to think outside the box when all I want is for you to know that *a bigger box exists*! Do you actually think that all of the financial elite were born with billions of dollars already in their cribs? No way. Actually, if you follow the Forbes 400 list of the richest people in the United States, you will see that most are actually self-made. In 2013, fifty-five of the top one hundred were. The average American believes that the deck is stacked and that there is very little chance of improving his or her financial standing. I want you to see beyond that limiting belief.

---

[21] Prince, *The Family Office,* 64

Do the "rules" of money keep the poor and middle class from succeeding? No. But you must be willing to educate yourself beyond traditional asset classes and the strategies you have heard of up until now. And who came up with these "rules," anyway? That's right—the government, the Federal Reserve, financial institutions, and large corporations. In other words, the status quo. Compliance with their rules benefits each of them, allowing them to profit from financial vehicles where you store your money or through your habits of consumption. They desire to control *access to your money.*

Here are a few myths or misperceptions that the status quo team has promoted about how we should make financial and money-related decisions:

- Financial security comes from working for a big company, saving in a 401k for retirement, and relying on the government to provide stability through entitlement programs.
- Stocks, bonds, and cash are the main asset classes that provide a highly diversified portfolio.
- You should focus on investment vehicles with the lowest expenses and immediate liquidity.
- Long-term investing is best done with traditional asset classes and a buy-and-hold strategy.
- If you want higher returns, you have to take more investment risks (the risk/return paradigm).
- FDIC protection makes banks your safest place to store money.
- You will likely be in a lower tax bracket at retirement so tax defer as much of your savings as possible.
- The definition of inflation is the rise in prices measured by the Consumer Price Index (CPI), and interest rates are tied to inflation rates.

These are just a few examples of common American beliefs about money that keep us from achieving our financial needs and wants.

When I researched how the financial elite approached their financial needs and wants, I came across two different types of financial institutions whose sole purpose is to use and maintain the money they oversee: pension plans and endowments. Both entities are structured to provide a stable flow of income to meet the needs of their beneficiaries. Many of you could be current or future recipients of pensions, although that type of plan is slowly becoming a distant memory. And an endowment is a pool of money—for example, a college or university draws from its endowment to benefit its students. While some endowments contain only a few million dollars, several of the top universities manage multibillion-dollar endowments. Two of the biggest—Harvard and Yale—have been extremely successful in their approaches to investing.

I reviewed the Yale Endowment Annual Report for 2012 and found some statements that I thought would be very interesting for individual investors to ponder. One was: "Yale employs investment and spending policies designed to preserve Endowment asset values while providing a substantial flow of income to the Operating Budget."[22] I asked myself, *Couldn't the same thing be said for individuals, families, and small business owners' financial priorities?*

And there's this statement:

> *Over the past twenty years, Yale significantly reduced the Endowment's exposure to traditional domestic marketable securities, reallocating assets to nontraditional asset classes. In 1992, over half of the Endowment was committed to U.S. stocks, bonds and cash. Today, domestic marketable securities account for approximately one-tenth of the portfolio and foreign equity, private equity, absolute return strategies and real assets represent nearly nine-tenths of the Endowment.[23]*

In fact, when you look at the Yale endowment's target allocation for each asset class, it paints a very different picture from the typical portfolio that an individual investor uses to try to diversify:

- Absolute return: 18 percent
- Domestic equity: 6 percent
- Fixed income: 4 percent
- Foreign equity: 8 percent
- Private equity: 35 percent
- Real estate: 22 percent
- Natural resources: 7 percent
- Cash: 0 percent

---

[22] Yale Endowment Annual Report, June 2012, 11
[23] Yale, 11

Yale explains that:

> The heavy allocation to nontraditional asset classes stems from the diversifying power they provide to the portfolio as a whole. Alternative assets, by their nature, tend to be less efficiently priced than traditional marketable securities, providing an opportunity to exploit market inefficiencies through active management. Today's portfolio has significantly higher expected returns and lower volatility than the 1992 portfolio.[24]

This type of portfolio positioning toward "alternative" assets can also be seen on a larger scale. According to the December 2010 report of the National Association of College and University Business Officers (NACUBO) and Commonfund Institute, here are the average allocations for endowments over $1 billion in assets:

- US stocks: 11 percent
- International stocks: 15 percent
- Fixed income: 10 percent
- Cash: 4 percent
- Alternatives: 60 percent

So if alternative asset classes (which are basically anything that isn't stocks, bonds, or cash) are desired by endowments and the financial elite, why don't more individual investors have them in their portfolios? Great question! I will address this topic in detail in the last couple of chapters. But before you can accomplish the task of properly allocating your money, we'll make sure you understand your *relationship with money* and how you are going to make money-related decisions that are in your best interest.

Educate. Empower. Enlighten.

---

[24] Yale, 12

Chapter 7: NLP—The Study of Excellence

Throughout my career, I have assisted hundreds of individuals, families, and small business owners in making sound, financially related decisions. Each client experience was unique because everyone has a different relationship with money. Since 2006, I have dedicated my time and energy toward educating myself about the science of neuro-linguistic programming because I believe NLP is a "difference maker" in our business model. Acknowledging our firm's understanding of NLP and its ability to help us make a deeper connection with our clients is a vital element to the remaining chapters in this book.

I want to challenge you to "think differently" about money and finance-related decisions. NLP can be a tool that assists you in your new paradigm of taking control of your financial picture and protecting your personal economy.

What is neuro-linguistic programming? NLP is a process of modeling our unique conscious and unconscious patterns to constantly move us toward higher potential. NLP is not a thing; it is a science that enlightens us about which actions work and how to repeat them to achieve continuing success.

Neuro means something to do with the brain. NLP considers our habits, good and bad. Most of our habits are stored in the unconscious mind. The key is to increase our awareness of those habits and then to shape them through conscious thought patterns. Learning to influence your own results can empower you toward both personal and business success.

Linguistic means something to do with language. NLP examines the verbal and nonverbal language that we use to communicate with ourselves (self-talk) and with others. Mastering the structure of our language is essential in a world where communication is at the heart of our daily lives.

Programming is the way in which we put patterns of thinking, language, and behavior together to get the results we deserve—good and bad. We run our lives with patterns or routines. Once you understand why you do what you do, you can begin to gain control of your unconscious as well as conscious intentions.

Why is NLP relevant in our discussion of money? Because NLP is really the study of how we get from an idea to an action to a desired result—and we can apply it to how we approach money. In fact, NLP is the study of *excellence*—and isn't that what we all want in our finances?

Sue Knight, author of *NLP at Work*, explains why NLP is so important today:

> We live in a world of unprecedented change. We are immersed in unpredictability and complexity. The more we discover, the more there is to discover. Every question reveals yet more questions. We need skills and attitudes to help us learn how to make sense of this chaos. When everything around us may seem to challenge who we are, we need to know how to find certainty within ourselves about what we want and what we believe. We need to take care of ourselves and stand alone in our self-assurance and empathy for others, yet we sometimes need to be able to show others our vulnerability and ask for help... We need the capacity to move more quickly than ever before... We need to know how to communicate with people of vastly different cultures and, more than anything, how to communicate with ourselves. We need to understand others' perceptions even if they are poles apart from ours; and we need to listen to the wisdom of our own bodies.[25]

I have studied the science of NLP since 2006, and through my work with Mike Lindstrom as a business coach, we have uncovered several fundamental pieces of NLP that can benefit each and every American who wants to protect his or her personal economy.

NLP Strategies: Modeling

Mike and I have found that the best way to benefit from NLP is to "model" someone who is really good at not only understanding the science but also at *implementing* the strategies to produce results. Isn't that what most investors are looking for when they work with a financial advisor or a firm—a business model with a proven track record that gets results and manages your expectations? The purpose of modeling talent in business is to reproduce excellence, yes. But you must realize that excellence is context specific. This means that a person can be excellent at something small, like part of a process,; or good at a whole system or some other sphere of action.

---

[25] Sue Knight, *NLP at Work*, Boston: Nicholas Brealy, 2012, 1–4

And NLP is an *active process*. The more you model excellence, the more you discover. NLP operates at a higher level than most traditional training. It helps you "learn how to learn." A frequent motto heard in NLP is: "If someone can do it, anyone can do it." This is the basis of modeling. It's the *how*.

Modeling develops a conscious awareness of a process, and with a conscious awareness, you have *choice*.

Mentoring

While beneficial, mentoring is not as useful as modeling because often the mentor doesn't know which is his or her most powerful skill or how he or she actually uses it. However, if the learner is equipped with NLP modeling skills then he or she can elicit the skills needed to learn. Be aware, however, that modeling does not recognize right versus wrong or positive versus negative. You can learn bad skills just as easily as good ones.

NLP is a way of "coding" excellence through the use of programs called *strategies*. It creates a process of decision making (that combines visual, auditory, and kinesthetic learning) and enables you to elicit context-specific patterns to reproduce excellence in your own unique environment.

Excellence

Individuals and organizations who consistently achieve the goals they set for themselves must pay attention to how they fit into the larger system of which they are a part. Their mission is to add value to the larger system—the entire organization—while retaining their own identities.

The Beliefs of Excellence

The following beliefs are important to living the concept of excellence:

- Each person is unique.
- Everyone makes the best choice available at the time.
- There is no failure—only feedback.
- Behind all behavior is a positive intention.
- The meaning of a communication is its effect (desired result).
- There is a solution to every problem.

- The person most flexible in thought and behavior has the best chance of succeeding.
- Mind and body are part of the same system.
- Knowledge, thought, memory, and imagination are the result of sequences and combinations of ways of filtering and storing information.

Capabilities of Excellence

Excellent people are sensitive toward themselves and others. They can recognize changes in their own and others' states and respond to such changes. They can change how and what they do when what they're doing isn't working. Finally, excellent people think in terms of outcomes. They can integrate their own outcomes and those of others (the *dovetailing* technique).

Behavior of Excellence

Excellent people act and speak every day in a way that aligns with their missions, their beliefs, and their capabilities. Their behavior is congruent, consistent, and free of mixed messages. They operate on a number of set principles that form the basis of everything they do.

Environment of Excellence

Excellent people recognize that their environments are expressions of who they are and what they think. They choose to be with people who and in places that share the same values, have common outcomes, and are engaged in the learning process.

A Path to Excellence

On your road to excellence, keep in mind that the map is not the territory. Most people tell you that you need to "think outside the box" or "get out of your comfort zone." What if all you needed was to know that a bigger box exists—and that getting out of your comfort zone just means growing and learning more as a human being? And always remember that "if you do what you always did, you get what you always got."

The Next Steps toward Excellence

A problem in the financial services industry is that the average person doesn't understand how working with an advisor or a firm can benefit his or her family. This lack of knowledge leads to the public's skepticism. They think we are just selling financial products to get commissions and are just taking advantage of our clients' money. Our own industry's incompetence contributes to the problem because we don't explain well how our services generate value: the financial services industry has an "explanation problem."

I believe that NLP techniques can help our industry immensely by making more financial advisors better business owners, yes, but I also see the need for the average American to grasp these concepts so that everyone is on the same page. The best way to accomplish this task is to explain to *both* audiences how NLP can teach people to think, communicate, and behave successfully regarding finance and money-related decisions.

Here are a few NLP principles and techniques that I have taught our firm's advisors to improve their comprehension of this science:

The Power of State and Physiology

People's current "states" influence how they receive information and experiences. Work on putting people in a positive or receptive state when you influence them.

Money is a stressful topic for many. Very few people feel comfortable openly talking about their past decisions (or indecisions) and what their needs and wants are when they meet with a financial professional. The meeting can be intimidating even if they understand what you are saying. Sometimes it can be helpful to remind the client, "I work for *you*," and "this is *your money* we are talking about, so you are in charge."

The Art of Framing (and Preframing)

Preframing is simply telling people what you are going to tell them before you tell them. Explain your expectations and desired results. The rest is up to them, but now they know what is going on.

This can put clients or prospects in the mindset you want them in. Should they be curious? Inquisitive? Ensure that every touch point with a prospect frames up the next steps or actions. Transform your initial consultation with a prospect, making sure that you strongly pre-frame *the* most important things you want them to walk away with—or that you remove any potential obstacles, objections, or concerns up front: "kill the monster while it is small."

When you pre-frame, you take away uncertainty and allow people's minds to focus on developing questions and process the information to see if it will fit their particular situations. For example, you could say, "Mr. and Mrs. Jones, today I would like to start off our presentation by explaining how we are different from other financial firms so you can determine if our process and philosophy can add value in your financial situation. I'd like to address any questions that you have afterward, and no matter what transpires in our conversation today, there is no expectation that you commit to working with us before you leave. Is this acceptable to you?"

The Power of Questions

When asking questions of people, it is important to "go deeper" in the conversation. My favorite metaphor to use here is that most people communicate in "shallow water." Why? Because that is a "safe" depth where you cannot get hurt. But we want to always go deeper and deeper in our questions to get to the "bottom of the ocean." This is where the real truth lies. This is where one's real pain and pleasure exist. Having the courage to go deeper is a skill set few financial professionals possess.

Understanding a client's relationship with money is vital to achieving any desired financial outcome, but very few financial professionals ever get into that subject. You need to know whether the client makes decisions from a past-, present-, or future-based mindset. Only powerful questions can unlock the answer.

Asking powerful questions also allows you to obtain vital "golden nuggets" of information—like kids' names, the date of the wedding anniversary, the client's interests, and so on. Always take copious notes (preferably in a professional-looking journal) when meeting with someone so you can extract and record these nuggets.

The key is to "personalize" the business relationship so that you can earn the *trust* of your clients. Most people assume that trust is given to financial professionals immediately because one allows them to participate in one's financial situation. A new or existing client may trust your *character*, but until a person has many positive experiences with you or your firm, your *competency* will always be in question. I educate my clients that every meeting with them is one more chance for me to "re-interview for my job," and that mindset keeps me searching for ways to add value (if only all people in service-oriented careers took that perspective).

Building a long-term, trusting relationship with a financial professional or an entire firm takes years, but the first ten minutes of your initial meeting should "set the table" in this direction. It could be as simple as answering the question, "Why are you here?" or "What caused you to want to meet with us today?" From that point forward, the conversation needs to be focused on *you* and how to create a customized approach to all of your needs and wants.

The financial professional needs to master the BENDWIMP (beliefs, evaluate, needs, desires/goals, wounds/fears, interests, proud of) method of probing for information through the use of thought-provoking, open-ended questions. Identifying at least two or three questions in each of the eight areas can make a huge difference in the client experience.

Setting Goals

Track specific, measurable activity: when setting your own goals and communicating them to a financial professional, check that all goals are "SMD" (specific, measurable, and dated). The more specific the goal, the easier it is to measure.

And always start with the outcome in mind when setting the goal. This helps eliminate fears and the influence of current life situations, setting the course for a big, bright future. Managing expectations must be a top priority for any financial professional because the one constant in anyone's financial picture is *change*.

So the clearer the picture you paint for the financial professional, the more customized the strategies he or she can recommend for you. However, very few people have a clear picture of what they want, so a financial professional well-trained in NLP techniques can assist you in this journey and be your guide as you take control of your financial picture.

Educate. Empower. Enlighten.

Chapter 8: How You Can Take Control of Your Financial Picture

A company's process should clearly illustrate how its business model differentiates it from every other firm. If a financial management company can demonstrate how it will educate you, implement strategies, communicate effectively, and manage your expectations then your decision to hire it (or not) will be simple. Remember, it's *your* money. You are in charge. The financial advisor or firm *works for you.* So be sure that your working relationship is a *fit.* You want to be comfortable with your advisor when you want long-term guidance for achieving the best long-term results.

The process we provide to our clients, and its elements, is very simple and straightforward. The key is to combine these elements with a powerful philosophy so that you can achieve financial freedom.

Education

> *We provide you information that helps you make decisions. We expand your knowledge base in areas beyond traditional asset classes. We introduce an environment that constantly searches for ways to add value.*

Numerous financial firms claim to focus on education. But which *specific* areas of finance and money-related information do they bring you? And is it *relevant*? Ask yourself: *Is the information they provide past-based only? Or is there present-based relevance and future-based guidance?* Their firm's philosophy is your guide for uncovering answers. After the firm educates you about its process and philosophy, do you feel yourself moving *toward* or *away from* making any decisions? If you are not being *challenged* to learn more about strategies and asset classes that are not mainstream or traditional, ask yourself this question: *does this lack of depth benefit my financial situation?*

Thirty years ago, the financial markets, the economy, investors, and average Americans were all focused on different priorities. There is no reason that your financial picture should be overseen by anyone who doesn't view the next thirty years as a *new frontier* in finance and money-related decisions. Why? Because things have changed dramatically over the past three decades. Adding value through education means developing a way to manage your expectations in a business relationship where you feel confident that your needs and wants are prioritized.

Confidence

I tell prospective clients all the time that our philosophy is not for everyone. But if our core principles are in line with your thinking, we can begin to focus on customized solutions. You should be confident:

- That our philosophy fits your mindset
- That you are clear on which of our services you want to utilize

Since your life doesn't happen in a straight line, you need to rely on an integrated resource network (IRN) to provide strategies and solutions where you need them the most. (I'll explain more about IRNs in chapter 9.) Until you're certain of your next financial move, it doesn't make sense to commit any of your resources (time, talent, or money). So achieving confidence is paramount if you want to make successful financial decisions.

Action

Deciding how to move forward with a financial strategy or vehicle can be very difficult. The alternative is to do nothing but remember that this is still a decision— and a very expensive one given the current change in the economy. How valuable is transparency in the information you consider in your financial decisions? It should be a priority for both you and your financial advisor because fees, expenses, liquidity restrictions, flexibility, and control of your investment dollars normally help determine which strategies *fit* your situation.

We recommend that you:

- Insist on transparent conversation with your financial advisor.
- Implement customized, one-size-fits-one strategies.
- Integrate as many resources as possible to simply your financial life.

The financial service industry has been tainted by unscrupulous individuals interested only in their own compensation, not their clients' interests. While those types of advisors are a small minority, and the rest of financial advisors keep their clients' needs ahead of their own, the public remains skeptical.

Trust

How do individuals, families, or small business owners overcome skepticism and build customized financial pictures that protect personal economy with someone they can *trust*? I believe that a firm's philosophy is the difference maker in today's uncertain economy. Just as a firm's process shows you *how* it will meet your expectations, the philosophy demonstrates *what* it will do to add value and earn the trust you expect from any of your financial professionals.

Trust has two crucial components: the *character* of the people you interact with concerning your money and their *competency* to measure and monitor your financial picture based on current economic conditions.

Simply put, you want to engage a financial advisor or a firm that is focused on providing *education* that creates *confidence* in your mind so that you can take *action* to achieve a relationship with your financial professional(s) based on *trust*. This is what education-based advising is all about—a process and philosophy that guide you toward *utilization* strategies and *protecting the purpose of your money*. You deserve this type of world-class communication—where information is shared in a timely manner to address your concerns and implement strategies that add value in your life.

A solid business model has a process that illustrates the day-to-day interaction with each client, but the heart of value creation lies in a cutting-edge philosophy. When these are properly explained to a client, the reaction should be a combination of confirmation, relief, desire to proceed, and possibly a touch of awe. Clients may wonder, *Why haven't I heard this type of information before?* Educate. Empower. Enlighten. A very important component to our process is making sure our clients understand that our motivation is to *serve first and add value in order to be compensated.* For clients to believe we are sincere in our motivation, educating them on the different methods of compensation is a must.

Note that to be compensated in the methods I describe here, an advisor must meet various requirements. Here are some examples as to how an advisor might commonly qualify:

- Be registered with the Financial Industry Regulatory Authority (FINRA), the major Self-Regulatory Organization (SRO) in the securities industry.

- Be registered with the state's insurance and securities departments (in each state where business is conducted).

- Hold the following licenses with the above-mentioned regulatory bodies:
  - Series 7
    - Allows the advisor access to more financial vehicles than a Series 6 alone
  - Series 63
    - Securities registration required by most states for commissionable sales
  - Series 65
    - An Investment Adviser Representative registration
    - Allows one to be compensated in ways other than commission
  - Series 66
    - An alternate license that combines the Series 63 and 65
  - Life and health insurance licenses in the client's state of residence

Please note: Other state insurance departments will offer reciprocity where an advisor is not required to take a different state's test, but they do require registration in that state.

Additional licenses can be obtained, as well as professional designations, depending on the advisor's areas of expertise and business focus. This is one of the main reasons I have been a proponent of working with a *team* of financial professionals because you will rarely find someone who can handle all areas of finance on his or her own.

How Do Financial Advisors Get Paid?

Financial advisors may be compensated in four different ways:

By the Hour or by Flat Fee

An advisor may be paid by the hour or by flat fee, either directly to the advisor by check or by debit from an investment account he or she oversees.

A signed engagement agreement normally outlines the hourly rate and the type of work that the client will receive upon completion. In most cases, such agreements involve the provision of information and education *only*—not the implementation of strategies or financial vehicles. The expectation is that clients handle those steps on their own. If the client desires that advisor to implement the strategies he or she recommends, the fees charged directly to the client are usually reduced or possibly eliminated because the advisor then receives compensation through another method. Make sure you clarify this point if you decide to work with a fee-only advisor.

By Asset-Based Management Fee

This fee is most common when you work with a fee-based advising firm. The compensation formula is pretty straightforward: the firm is paid a set percentage of your assets under management (AUM) with the firm. This fee may equate to 1 percent average AUM, but it could vary based on the firm's business model.

In this case, the firm is being compensated to make investment recommendations regarding your portfolio allocation as well as any other services it provides. Ideally, this management fee will end up being paid by the growth on your assets:

Total Performance	Advisor Compensation	Impact on Client's Account
Portfolio grows by 5 percent.	Advisor receives 1 percent.	The client keeps 4 percent.

(The client keeps 80 percent of the growth.)

Total Performance	Advisor Compensation	Impact on Client's Account
Portfolio grows by 10 percent.	Advisor receives 1 percent.	The client keeps 9 percent.

(The client keeps 90 percent of the growth.)

Total Performance	Advisor Compensation	Impact on Client's Account
Portfolio grows by 20 percent.	Advisor receives 1 percent.	The client keeps 19 percent.

(The client keeps 95 percent of the growth.)

As you can see, the fee-based advising model focuses on *accumulation* and *performance-based results.* But don't lose sight of the amount of *risk* in the portfolio because losses to your portfolio do not normally change the advisor's compensation. In other words, let's say that your portfolio drops 10 percent. The advisor still receives the 1-percent management fee.

Total Performance	Advisor Compensation	Impact on Client's Account
Portfolio declines by 10 percent.	Advisor receives 1 percent.	The client loses 11 percent.

So the portfolio actually drops by 11 percent. The advisor is always earning revenue no matter what impact the investment performance (or lack thereof) has on your financial picture.

Because this method of compensation is usually driven by the way the client's portfolio is constructed, I've found it vitally important to the long-term advisor-client relationship to provide additional resources to clients beyond just investment management. Since no advisor or firm controls how the market or investments will perform in the future, I usually recommend that an advisor's compensation not be solely tied to this method.

By Commission on the Amount Invested

The commission method is usually seen as *transactional* in nature because when a commission is paid to an advisor, the money comes directly out of the client's invested principal.

For example, a client invests ten thousand dollars into an individual security (like a stock). Assume that a commission of 3 percent is charged up front to new investors. Out of the ten-thousand-dollar investment, ninety-seven hundred dollars goes to work in the investment chosen, and three hundred dollars is paid to the advisor's firm.

In certain situations, this type of compensation can actually *benefit* the client's financial picture because the commissionable product may have an effectively lower cost as money accumulates over time. If a client's purpose for these particular monies is to generate growth through income, it may make sense to lower any long-term expenses associated with the strategy.

One of the main fears of this method is that when advisors are compensated up front, they may have no desire to keep adding value for the client. I understand this perspective, but I like to remind clients that there is a difference between a salesperson and an advisor. This compensation method should not make you feel as though you were *sold* an investment. Instead, the financial vehicle you implement should be based on its appropriateness in your financial picture.

Financial Institutions As Intermediaries

Our financial institutions offer hundreds of financial products and services. Most banks, brokerage firms, insurance companies, and other financial intermediaries offer the public in-house advisors or salaried employees. The same products and services can be accessed through independent advisors. Certain companies may promote their own proprietary products to in-house advisors and provide additional compensation for those products, which creates a conflict of interest where it's possible that the advisor's interests are put ahead of the client's. Of course, I could be a little biased toward independent advisors since I've spent my entire eighteen-year career in that space. However, I like to approach this topic from a factual position because I've met many high-quality advisors who take great care of their clients, and they come from all backgrounds. Again, transparency and open communication about compensation and suitability are vital to managing a client's expectations.

A question I get from a lot of clients is, "How is this method of compensation different from receiving a commission?" One difference is that when you choose to implement a financial vehicle through an intermediary (including annuities, life insurance contracts, or non-traded real estate investment trusts [REITs], to name a few), 100 percent of your invested principal goes to work for you inside the financial vehicle. The compensation is coming directly from the financial institution's marketing budget. This makes sense to the institution because its financial vehicle is not going to sell itself. An experienced financial professional has to assess your needs and determine if the particular vehicle is a fit for your financial picture. Plus the advisor needs to maintain a continuous relationship with clients, monitoring any changes in their situations that may impact the validity of the financial vehicle.

Now it's important to realize that just because the advisor is getting paid by the financial institution, it doesn't mean the product or vehicle is *free*. The advisor's compensation is part of any and all fees, expenses, and restrictions placed on the design of the financial vehicle. This is no different from a real estate transaction in which you use a buyer's agent. If the home sells for $300,000, who pays your buyer agent the 3-percent compensation for assisting you? The seller. The cost of the home does not change; you are still getting it for $300,000. The seller just receives 94 percent of the sale price ($282,000) at closing if the seller's agent also gets 3-percent commission.

If the client knows all of the fees and expenses associated with the financial vehicle, how the financial institution chooses to pay the advisor becomes a nonfactor—assuming there is transparency and open communication.

Even though each client's personal economy is unique, the financial vehicles that are suitable to create customized, one-size-fits-one solutions may be similar in an advisor's practice. Based on the advisor's comfort level with certain financial institutions or his/her expertise in certain strategies, it's possible that several clients could benefit from owning similar products or implementing similar strategies. Also, an advisor's or firm's total compensation can come from more than one of the four methods; there is no set formula for how an advisor should get paid. That determination is between the client and the advisor. In addition, the agreement can evolve over time as the client-advisor relationship grows.

Finally, remember that there are no such things as perfect investments or ideal financial strategies. All that matters is that the financial vehicle(s) implemented is *appropriate* for your current financial picture and that you are satisfied with how your advisor is interacting with you to earn his or her compensation.

Educate. Empower. Enlighten.

Chapter 9: What You Can Do to Protect Your Personal Economy

Our firm's advance-and-protect philosophy is different from other philosophies in the financial service industry that many savers and investors have embraced. "Hope" is not an investment strategy, yet it is a core component of the buy-and-hold mentality that has influenced most people in the past three decades. With advance and protect, we are proactive in managing your entire savings portfolio—all the time.

I would like to explain the separate components and then illustrate ways you can protect your personal economy with this knowledge.

The four pillars of our advance-and-protect philosophy each play integral roles in helping our advisors add value in serving their clientele. We:

Diversify Your Risk Using Alternative Asset Classes

Most individual investors put their money to work in traditional asset classes (stocks, bonds, and cash). They are still exposed to the risks of market volatility, inflation, taxes, and longevity. For decades, however, pension plans, endowments, financial institutions, and wealthy individuals have managed *their* portfolios using alternative investments in an effort to help minimize or mitigate these risks.

We intend to educate our clients on the institutional mindset and provide them with information on how they can access these same types of asset classes and financial strategies. While diversification cannot ensure a profit or protect against a loss, we help you diversify your investment portfolios using various non-correlated asset classes to help minimize your risk.

Implement Tax Diversification of Your Assets

Minimizing income tax is an important part of planning your financial future. Every dollar of taxes you save is one more dollar you can save or spend in the future. Our advisors work with you to help ensure you have a balance of taxable, tax-deferred, and tax-exempt assets—that's tax diversification—so that you can use your money effectively. Many financial firms fail to coordinate the strategies of risk diversification with tax diversification of assets. We believe you cannot perform one without the other if you want to achieve financial balance in your life.

Protect the Purpose of Your Money

You cannot control what happens in this economy, but you can control how you respond to the changes and protect the purpose of your money. We believe there are no such things as good or bad investments or products; it's all about the appropriateness of the financial vehicles that help prioritize what we call our "safety, liquidity, growth" model.

•**Safety:** Learn strategies that can help you protect your principal or the income it generates.

•**Liquidity:** We provide guidance about how to get access to your money when you need it.

•**Growth:** We help you strategize and determine your money's growth "profile" through either income (interest, dividends, and yield) sources or appreciation (an increase in security price to be reinvested or sold in the future for a gain).

Since there is no perfect investment, the key is to balance these characteristics with each pool of money that you plan to use, whether for month-to-month expenses or savings for big-ticket items.

Coordinate Every Piece of Your Financial Picture

As members of an independent firm, our advisors make decisions based on what's best for our clients, not on preferred relationships or on how we are compensated. Each partner throughout our integrated financial resources network understands our advance-and-protect philosophy and works together to provide you with products and services that best fit your situation.

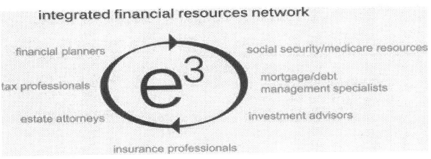

Note: Services provided by estate attorneys, health/LTC insurance and mortgage specialists are offered by a third party and NPC does not provide tax, Social Security or Medicare services.

Here are some questions to consider:

- When was the last time your investment advisor asked to see your income tax return?
- Are your tax professionals *proactive* with income tax strategies, or do they just *react* to the information you provide them every year?
- How should you structure your mortgage in retirement? Should you just pay it off?
- Is your investment portfolio designed for accumulation or utilization?
- Has anyone looked at your options for Social Security benefits or Medicare coverage and helped you decide which decisions you should make in your personal economy?
- What options do you have to help protect your assets from medical issues or long-term care needs?
- Are all of your accounts properly titled and have the right beneficiaries for an efficient transfer of your estate?

Nowadays, so much uncertainty exists within our educational system, housing market, employment, and health care arenas that it's up to you to protect your personal economy. You need a team of financial professionals who are experts in all areas that deal with money. Proactive strategies that simplify your financial life are essential.

Minimizing Risk

A philosophy that focuses on minimizing certain risks in a client's financial picture is not revolutionary by itself. It is the prioritizing of risk minimization that has completely changed the paradigm of the financial service industry over the past thirty years. As you review this section, ask whether you see the following risks impacting your personal economy over the next one to ten years.

Market Volatility

The Dow Jones Industrial Average and the S&P 500 Index reached all-time highs in 2013. Does that give you confidence in the market and the economy? Do you wonder how the market achieved those all-time highs? Has your portfolio benefitted from the last few years of the stock market's climb, or have you been on the sidelines, waiting for the "right" moment to get back into the market?

If your financial advisors are not educating you about the reasons behind the recent stock market performance and its future potential then you need to get a second opinion. The same thing goes for any bond or other fixed-income holdings you have now. We are in uncharted territory for bonds; it's beyond most people's actual investment experience. Over the last thirty years, interest rates have decreased, allowing bonds to actually outperform stocks (measured by thirty-year treasury bonds versus the S&P 500 Index). Unfortunately, as I've noted, this performance cannot be duplicated in the near future because increasing interest rates will punish the values of bond holders' principal. You need a proactive strategy that can address this economic reality and a firm that can offer you solutions, not excuses.

Inflation

Do you believe that the government's measure of inflation, the Consumer Price Index, accurately reflects what affects your situation? Does it bother you that things like most food and gas are not included in the current CPI calculation? The *true* definition of inflation relates to the devaluation of our currency. The more money the Federal Reserve prints, the less "stuff" you can buy with a dollar. What should really matter to you is how your personal economy is impacted by real inflation. If the stuff you buy is getting more expensive, you need to make sure your money is working for you to offset that change in your purchasing power.

Taxes

Simple question: do you think taxes will go down, stay the same, or go up in the future? The US government collected a record amount of tax revenue in 2013, and it helped reduce the budget deficit almost by half. However, there is no indication that the government plans to eliminate its budget deficits or dependence on debt. If anything, a future boost in tax revenues will just allow it to spend more. Remember that you are only required to pay taxes on your money *once*! Implement strategies that tax diversify your assets so you can take control of your financial picture.

Longevity

Good news: as a society, we are living longer. Bad news: we are living longer. For the past thirty years, people have been using traditional asset classes to build up their nest eggs, and that has allowed millions of Americans to get *to* retirement safely. But now what?

The game is just beginning. You are only at halftime, and a good locker-room talk is way overdue for most savers who see their stock holdings fluctuating, their bond yields dropping, and their bank accounts paying minimal interest. The strategies you implemented to *accumulate* your wealth were from a time when the US economy was growing and people had confidence that our government would do what was in the best interest of our citizens. Please don't wait for someone else to figure these things out for you. The time is now because we do not know what tomorrow has in store for any of us.

Alternative Asset Classes as Financial Vehicles

We've noted that asset classes and financial vehicles exist beyond the traditional stock, bond, and cash options. In chapter 6 we discussed how the financial elite favor alternative asset classes and work with family offices to manage them. Institutions such as pension plans and endowments also hold a majority of their portfolios in alternative asset classes. While I would enjoy the opportunity to educate you regarding several different types of alternative asset classes, unfortunately this book is not the proper forum.

As a licensed securities representative of an independent broker-dealer, I am restricted by regulatory bodies (such as FINRA and the SEC) to discuss asset classes such as private equity, hedge funds, real assets, currencies, managed futures, non-traded real estate investment trusts (REIT), business development companies (BDC), master limited partnerships (MLP) or unit investment trusts (UIT) without a prospectus and proper disclosures. Alternative investments can be speculative in nature, and may not be suitable for all investors. The strategies employed in the management of such investments involve certain increased risks, including lack of liquidity and the potential loss of part or the entire principal amount invested.

Realize that what matters at this time is how each asset class or financial vehicle can assist you in minimizing different risks through its characteristics and protect the purpose of your money. All asset classes and financial vehicles have different structures that impact fees, expenses, restrictions on liquidity, and control as well as benefits to your financial picture.

The key to this section is *not* in attempting to determine right now which asset classes are appropriate for you. I simply want to expand your knowledge: *that a bigger box of financial tools exists.* Learning more about these different asset classes may cause you to desire a meeting with a competent financial advisor or firm that has expertise in these areas. There are a few alternative asset classes I can mention briefly to get you on the path of thinking differently.

Owning a Business

Owning your own business may appear a risky way to make a living. But if you begin to understand the flexibility and control that business owners have over their financial pictures, you may change your mind. One of my passions is to assist my clients who want to become more entrepreneurial in the utilization of their personal economies. (Toward the end of chapter 10, I will share information that can help you see the proper mindset necessary to manage your financial picture just like a successful CEO.)

Annuities

Annuities seem to be a polarizing topic whenever they are mentioned in a conversation. Some people have had positive experiences owning some type of annuity in their portfolio, while others may have a negative perspective on annuities. In this section, I have chosen to use Investopedia as an objective third party to provide a general definition of an annuity and its structure.

Investopedia defines an annuity as follows:

> *A financial product sold by financial institutions that is designed to accept and grow funds from an individual and then, upon annuitization, pay out a stream of payments to the individual at a later point in time. Annuities are primarily used as a means of securing a steady cash flow for an individual during retirement.*
>
> *Annuities can be structured according to a wide array of details and factors, such as the duration of time that payments from the annuity can be guaranteed to continue. Not all annuities must be annuitized. In fact, there*

are several forms of annuities that provide a period when the owner can walk away with the contract value. This is called the surrender period.[26]

The different ways in which annuities can be structured provide owners the flexibility to construct an annuity contract that will best meet their needs. You can add riders or benefits to these contracts to enhance their risk minimization capabilities. And while several types of annuities exist, the details on their differences are beyond the scope of this book. Any decision made to implement a financial vehicle requires a conversation with an experienced advisor who understands the benefits, features, fees, and expenses associated with various annuity contracts.

Life Insurance Contracts

Investopedia says that a permanent life insurance contract is

> A type of life insurance policy that pays out upon the policyholder's death, and also accumulates value during the policyholder's lifetime. Policyholders can use the cash value as a tax-sheltered investment (the interest and earnings on the policy are not taxable), as a fund from which to borrow and as a means to pay policy premiums later in life, or they can pass it on to their heirs. There are several types of cash-value life insurance. Cash-value insurance is also known as permanent life insurance because it provides coverage for the policyholder's entire life.

> The other major category of life insurance is called term insurance because it is generally in force only for a term of ten to thirty years or until the policyholder cancels it. Cash-value insurance has higher premiums than term insurance because part of the premium pays for the death benefit coverage, and part of it goes toward the policy's cash value. Cash-value life insurance is often criticized because investment options may be limited and not as good as what an investor could get on his or her own.[27]

For the purposes of this book, I look at life insurance as an asset class. This means that we focus on the characteristics of permanent life insurance to help our clients minimize risk in their financial pictures. This type of policy is designed a specific way to meet the specifications of the IRS and the insurance companies.

[26] "Definition of an Annuity," http://www.investopedia.com/terms/a/annuity.asp
[27] "Definition of Life Insurance," http://www.investopedia.com/terms/l/life-insurance.asp

Also, please understand that with this type of policy, we are not talking about investing your money in the traditional sense. Rather, we are talking about *creating a system of financing*. Financing is a *process*, not a product. Financing involves the creation of, the maintenance of, and the use of a pool of money: all three simultaneously. When the system combines reduced income tax liability with a financing engine, it allows you better control over your capital.

It's amazing to me that the general public doesn't understand that the very purpose of insurance companies is to minimize risk for their customers—and make their profit from that worthwhile endeavor. The actual structure of annuities and life insurance contracts means that you are *transferring certain risks to the insurance company for a cost so that your financial picture is protected.* Common sense should tell you that if the purpose of part of your portfolio is to provide safety (of your principal or income deriving therefrom) and growth through income-first strategies, looking at vehicles provided by insurance companies could assist you in taking control of your financial picture.

At this point the risk of income taxes needs to be addressed separately because the IRS's tax treatment of each asset class is different, and it also depends on which type of account you store the money in. This risk is rarely addressed by financial advisors either because they lack the expertise in tax strategy implementation or it isn't a service they deem worthy to offer their clients. Rather, they choose to focus on performance and the accumulation of your money. But remember, most people don't save money so it can just sit there. They want to *use* it!

Individuals, families, and small business owners use their money for the two main purposes we discussed in chapter 4: month-to-month expenses are the *needs*, while the big-ticket items represent the *wants*. I have yet to meet a client who is satisfied to just meet needs and pay bills. The reason behind all of a saver's good money habits is to achieve the wants of life *while simultaneously meeting his or her needs.*

The way your money will be taxed at withdrawal is something you should be aware of *before* you need or want access to your stored money. Maybe I'm crazy, but I've always believed that the focus should be on how much money you keep from your financial endeavors, not how much you make. Make sense to you? If so, you really need to align yourself with a firm that prioritizes the minimization of risk in your financial picture—now more than ever with the threats of market volatility, inflation, and taxes to those savers and investors who have done a great job of creating their wealth. Agreed?

Now what about longevity risk—running out of money before you run out of time? This risk has crept into retirees' (or potential retirees') mindsets over the past ten to fifteen years. They've watched the economic headwinds build and the rosy optimism in our society turn into pragmatic realism concerning fundamental problems with our country's financial health. As more Americans turn to the government and the rest of the status quo for answers, they seem to be content with kick-the-can-down-the-road solutions and the inevitable creation of an entitlement society that traps several generations of Americans to come.

But wait! This result is not predestined for everyone. You have the capability to protect your personal economy and address the concerns of longevity risk. How is this possible, you ask? You can proactively implement strategies that primarily diversify your portfolio with asset classes that generate growth through income first. This is not a new concept. Back in the 1940s and 1950s, more than 60 percent of the total growth created by the S&P 500 Index was made up of *dividends*. So a traditional portfolio met this goal automatically. These days, dividends yield the S&P 500 Index comprise about 20-30 percent because there is a greater focus on appreciation with stock investing today.[28] That is fine for those who are still accumulating assets, but when you are ready to live on them, your risks are magnified. Alternative asset classes can help you address many of these risks.

Think about this scenario for a moment: let's say you and your financial advisor have analyzed your financial picture as you near retirement or that you're retired and seek to maintain your current lifestyle. You agree that achieving a 6- to 8-percent portfolio growth gives you a high probability of keeping your lifestyle intact (same month-to-month expenses and big-ticket items) and still have assets to pass on to your heirs. Assuming you have a balanced portfolio of stocks, bonds, and cash holdings, it is very possible that your portfolio looks like this:

Equities: 50 percent
- 30 percent US large cap
- 10 percent US mid-to-small cap
- 10 percent international/emerging markets

---

[28] "S&P 500 Dividend Yield – Historical Figures" http://www.multpl.com/s-p-500-dividend-yield/

Bonds/Cash: 50 percent
- 20 percent US investment-grade corporate bonds
- 10 percent US high-yield corporate bonds
- 10 percent US government bonds
- 10 percent cash

I see this scenario frequently with prospective clients who are referred to me or who listen to my radio show. Their question to me is, "Can I make it *through* retirement with this type of portfolio?" My response to them is always that I have no idea! I don't know how each of those asset classes will perform over the next ten, twenty, thirty years. So, why did an allocation of stocks, bonds and cash make sense to individual investors for the past 30+ years? You need to consider the perspective of investors during that time period. The main risk people focused on minimizing was market volatility and nothing else was prioritized.

Inflation was rarely discussed as the early 1980's became a distant memory due to declining interest rates and intervention by the Federal Reserve. Also, the public was (and still is) misled in understanding the true definition of inflation – which is the devaluation of our currency. Confusion led people to believe interest rate movements are a *cause* of inflation versus a *signal* to the market as how to properly allocate capital. The impact of taxes on someone's financial picture wasn't a concern because the majority of Americans believed they would be in a lower tax bracket in retirement and thus began the process of tax-deferring as much of their monthly savings as possible!

The Revenue Act of 1978 created the laws that govern 401k plans and they came into vogue in the 1980's as major corporations began adding them to their benefit packages alongside defined benefit pension plans. Eventually 401k plans and other defined contribution programs replaced most pensions and shifted longevity risk back to the employee. Realize that longevity risk (the fear of running out of money) is a recent phenomenon for retirees. Not because the risk is "new" but rather because of the breakdown in the "Three-Legged Stool" of retirement planning (pensions, social security and personal savings). As people retired in the 1980's, 1990's, and early 2000's they could rely on a company pension and social security benefits to cover the bulk of their lifestyle needs. The rest of their needs and wants were achieved through utilization of their savings. Because their savings were well-diversified in some mixture of stocks, bonds and cash, they could live as they always dreamed without major worries off their CD interest, muni-bond yields or consistent dividends from their blue-chip stocks.

Now what happens when the "traditional system" breaks down? Stocks become more volatile, so you become more conservative. Bonds and Cash asset classes cannot provide you the income you were previously accustomed to because interest rates have dropped to all-time lows. Everyday living expenses increase in cost and you begin to experience real inflation through the loss of purchasing power with the US dollar. The Financial Crisis of 2007-2008 impacts all areas of your life – family, neighbors, your company, the city you live in, the government you have trusted will take care of you and the government begins to make tough choices that create "winners and losers" financially. Healthcare becomes a major issue for families and retirees. Not because of the new laws but rather when people start realizing they may live longer in retirement than the number of years they actually worked and saved money! How does an individual, family or an entrepreneur plan for the unexpected when they are provided with limited knowledge and resources on these important areas of money and finance?

With the right philosophy guiding your financial advisor or firm, I believe that you can achieve the daunting task of protecting your personal economy. Some firms may educate you on *parts* of the philosophy I described. The question I have for you is: do you want your financial picture exposed to the risks I've discussed and your strategies to fall short due to a lack of access to all of the resources you require? If your answer is no then you should not settle for less than you deserve— even if it means working with another advisor or complementing your existing team with new resources. Remember, this is *your* money. Do what you need to do so you can achieve financial freedom.

Educate. Empower. Enlighten.

Chapter 10: Thinking and Acting Differently with Your Financial Home

When prospective clients come into my office and tell me about their experiences with other advisors or firms, many times they share frustrations. For some reason, a lot of financial professionals attempt to push their own agendas on clients. So to help get the prospective client on the right track, I ask them a simple question: "Whose money is this?"

It's yours, obviously! So the agenda should also be yours. Your advisor needs to understand how you think, feel, and act when it comes to finance and money-related decisions so he or she can add value to your financial picture. This means that your initial appointment should focus on one priority: *defining your personal economy.*

Defining Your Personal Economy

To understand your current needs, wants, and risks at the present stage of your life, you should expect a series of questions that gauge the level of resources you require to meet your expectations. To help you hear what that process would ideally sound like, I have composed a list of questions that help our advisors work through our process and philosophy with individuals, families, and small business owners.

The first set of questions is open-ended. The purpose is for you to share your experiences, past, present, and future, regarding your personal economy.

I begin with, "What would you like to accomplish in the time we spend together today?"

I like to remind my clients all the time: "It's your money. I work for *you*. I am your guide on this financial journey, but you need to tell me what's on your mind to get things started." This way, whatever agenda they have can take priority. Then I ask:

- What keeps you up at night (if anything) about your money?
- What are your worries about the economy?
- What was money like for you growing up?

These questions go together. Clients need to talk about what is *holding them back from achieving financial freedom.* Most of the time, the emotional side of investing and saving gets in the way of achieving their goals. So it's important for the advisor to understand *why the clients think about money the way they do.* People are driven to take action based on either avoiding pain or seeking pleasure. Your advisor needs to determine whether your priority is to move away from the pain (e.g. loss of your principal because of stock market turbulence) or move toward the pleasure (e.g. financial freedom). Neither scenario is right or wrong; you just need to know which method you want to use.

Here are more key questions:

- What are you looking for in an advisor?
- How much risk are you comfortable with in your financial picture?
- What would have to happen for you to be ecstatic about your financial progress over the next three, five, and ten years?
- What is your "definition" of retirement?
- Describe your ideal day in retirement.

Now we are getting into the specifics of your personal economy. The answers to these questions help shape how an advisor communicates information to you, which methods of decision making are best suited to your personality, and how to manage your expectations. When you are lost and look at a map, you need to find two points—where you are and where you want to go. The answers to these questions provide clarification on both of those points. Your advisor's priority is a successful transition between those two points knowing that no two clients experience the same journey.

Once this information is gathered, it is important to get a *snapshot* of your specific financial picture. Below, you will find the elements to a financial picture that our firm believes every single advisor should have a working knowledge of for their clients. When a complete financial picture is put together, constructing a customized, one-size-fits-one solution is much easier.

The Elements of a Financial Picture

The questions below are about the information you provide the advisor about the specifics of your financial picture:

- Who influences you the most when you make financial decisions?
- Do you seek any investment advice from the person(s) listed on your account statements?
- What do you like about your current investment decisions?

Your advisor needs to understand which resources you currently use and which roles they play in your financial decisions. The intent is that the new resources *complement* those you already find valuable, not replace them. And ideally you should have an inner circle of trusted advisors—a group with a broad selection of expertise who communicate with each other regularly.

- What is the purpose of the money in each of your accounts?

Simply put, if an advisor knows the purpose of each pool of your money, he or she can create solutions that protect those purposes and assist you in taking control of your financial picture.

- Can I see your most recent quarterly account statements?

Clients often have a certain level of financial illiteracy. Advisors should verify which types of accounts you have, the legal ownership of each, and whether what you think is in your accounts matches reality.

- What is your savings account balance?
- Do you keep it steady, add to it, or withdraw from it for spending?

Your answer provides a glimpse of your save/spend pattern with respect to cash flow and opens up the conversation about strategies to assist you in controlling the flow of your money.

- What do you feel our next steps should be?

At the end of the appointment, your advisor should take direction from you. Protecting your personal economy is a two-way street. You need to *buy into* the process and philosophy for it to be successful. Your thoughts and guidance about the next steps are crucial.

Example Strategies

Let's look at an example so you can get a sense of the types of strategies we provide for our clients. The layout of the example contains all of the required information in a client's financial picture. It's important that a complete financial picture is obtained in every client situation so as to make sure a customized one-size-fits-one approach is taken.

Our sample clients are both age sixty-five and preparing to retire very soon. They have $1 million in assets plus pensions and Social Security benefits.

The Clients' Savings and Investments

First, we looked at the asset classes in the clients' portfolio. Not surprisingly, they follow the lines of a traditional portfolio:

$500,000 in US Equities/Stocks
$400,000 in US Bonds/Fixed Income
$100,000 in Cash/CD's/Money Market

For tax diversification of assets, we consider the following types of accounts:

Taxable assets
- o Any account that sends a 1099 for interest, dividends, or capital gains
- o Bank (savings, money market, CDs), brokerage, and trust accounts

Tax-deferred accounts
- o Qualified plans (401k, IRA, 403b, and other retirement plans)
- o Nonqualified plans (certain annuities and 457 deferred-compensation plans)
- o Certain assets that defer taxes until liquidation (real estate, a business)

Tax-exempt assets and accounts
- o Home equity
- o Assets that provide tax-advantaged income
- o Roth IRA
- o Life insurance cash values

Our example couple has the following tax diversification:

Taxable
  o $100,000 in bank accounts paying less than 1-percent interest
  o $100,000 in brokerage account (various stock and bond investments)
Tax-deferred
  o $500,000 in 401k plan
  o $200,000 in various traditional IRAs
Tax-exempt
  o $100,000 in Roth IRAs

Cash Flow

Cash flow is the lifeblood of a household but very few Americans pay close attention to their saving/spending habits. Even the word "budget" makes some people cringe...and they could actually be in really good shape financially. Our firm wants to educate our clients to build a *spending awareness* that identifies your income sources as well as your financial needs and wants.

Here are the main items for us to identify:

Money IN
  o If you are still working:
      o Take-home pay (W2 or 1099)
          ▪ Weekly (52 x), biweekly (26 x), bimonthly (24 x), or monthly (12 x)
      o Bonuses or distributions from your business (K-1)
      o Rental income or other passive investments
  o If you are retired or want to retire:
      o Pension benefits
      o Social Security benefits
      o Rental income or other passive investments
Money OUT
  o Lifestyle (your needs: paying the bills)
  o Big-ticket items (your wants: for enjoyment)
  o Taxes (factored separately for retirees)
  o Additional line items
      o Health care
      o Family's and dependents' needs

- o A set savings contribution
- o Accelerated debt repayment

Our sample clients have three main sources of income:

1. Pension benefits (both spouses)
2. Social Security benefits (both spouses)
3. $1,000,000 in assets to cover the gap between money in and money out

Budget (Cash Flow) - Current Situation			
Based on Monthly Figures			
Name/Source	IN		OUT
Pension at Age 65	$	2,000	
Pension at Age 65	$	500	
SS Benefits at Age 65	$	2,000	
SS Benefits at Age 65	$	1,000	
LIFESTYLE			$ 7,000
BIG TICKET ITEMS			$ 1,000
INCOME TAXES			$ 1,500
Total:	$	5,500	$ 9,500
FROM ASSETS:	$	4,000	
% of ASSETS:		4.80%	

The clients desire ninety-five hundred dollars ($9,500) per month to meet their lifestyle needs and wants. We also factor in an estimate of their federal and state income taxes. Pensions and Social Security benefits will cover fifty-five hundred dollars ($5,500) of the required monthly income, or almost 60 percent of the clients' financial picture (and almost 80 percent of their lifestyle expenses). Another way to look at it is that sixty-six thousand dollars ($66,000) of annual income will be provided via two institutions (the federal government and the particular corporations that the clients worked for over several years). Therefore, part of their longevity risk is *transferred* to those institutions. As long as the government and companies remain solvent, this income is essentially guaranteed. This is a common scenario for Americans who have done a good job of saving for retirement.

The traditional "three-legged stool" is in good shape for these clients...so far. Now all they need to figure out is how best to generate four thousand dollars each month from the $1 million of assets in their portfolio. That equates to 4.80 percent of annual withdrawals from their assets.

In other words, if there's a negative difference between income sources (money in) and one's needs and wants (money out) in retirement, income from assets will need to make up "the gap" each month. The percentage it must generate is the target amount of *growth through income first* and determines which investment strategies to consider.

The lower the percentage you need (0 to 5 percent), the greater the possibility that your personal economy can be insulated from all risks (market volatility, inflation, taxes, and longevity). If your assets need to generate a higher percentage (6 percent or more), various risks may come into play because you will need further assistance from these assets. They'll have to produce *growth through appreciation* as well as income. A higher percentage of need may also mean you should delay retirement and continue saving to bring the percentage to a reasonable figure. Or you may decide to adjust your needs and/or wants to make retirement a reality.

This mindset is completely different from that of most financial advisors and their traditional portfolio designs. They would have you think of your assets as a big bucket of money from which you simply draw out a set amount or percentage. In their model, the withdrawals come out of the *bottom of the bucket*, and your growth is added back into the *top of the bucket*.

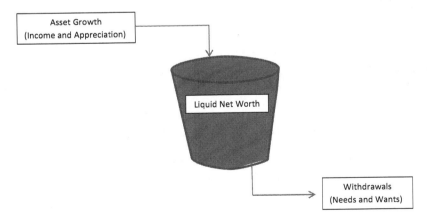

As long as you don't run out of money in the bucket, you are okay. Unfortunately, this method does not factor in risk minimization, tax strategies, or the purpose of your money (needs versus wants). If you use it, you are completely overlooking ways to take control of your financial picture and protect your personal economy.

Your Tax Return

Here are the main items we like to review on a client's tax return. (Of course, everyone's tax return will have unique sets of numbers, and some returns are much more complicated, but here I use a simple example that broadly applies.) We'll consider:

- o Adjusted gross income
- o Itemized or standard deduction
- o Exemptions (including for any dependents)
- o Which marginal tax bracket currently applies

2013 Tax Return		
Adjusted Gross Income:	$	114,000
Standard or Itemized Deduction	$	16,000
Exemptions:	$	7,800
Taxable Income:	$	90,200
Income Taxes:	$	14,408
Effective Tax:		12.6%

2013 MARGINAL TAX BRACKETS	
$425,000 and Over	$125,846 + 39.6%
$398,350 to $425,000	$107,768.50 + 35%
$223,050 to $398,350	$49,919.50 + 33%
$146,400 to $223,050	$28,457.50 + 28%
$72,500 to $146,400	$9,982.50 + 25%
$17,850 to $72,500	$1,785 + 15%
$0 to $17,850	10%
Filing Status:	Married Filing Jointly

To minimize the impact of taxes, you must realize how all of the components can work together in your favor.

This example assumes a standard deduction and two personal exemptions. While the $90,200 in taxable income puts this client in the 25-percent marginal tax bracket, the more important calculation is the effective tax rate: 12.6 percent. This means that for every dollar of income in 2013, 12.6 cents went to federal taxes (based on 2013 figures). No taxes are owed on the first $23,800 of taxable income because of the available deductions and exemptions. Also, we used a 6-percent state tax rate here since most of our clients are in the state of Missouri, but of course your state tax may be different.

Note that not every client's income tax situation can be significantly improved. A client's occupation, assets, sources of income, and how many expenses are deductible are just a few items that must be researched. What every individual, family, and small business owner needs to understand, though, is that *every dollar saved in taxes is one more dollar they can spend or save in the future.* Integrating proactive income tax strategies should be a priority when choosing your relationship with a financial professional.

Next, I want to share with you some areas we provide value to our clients using this example. You need to see for yourself how our advance-and-protect philosophy can come alive for potential clients in their sixties who have important finance and money-related decisions to make over the rest of their lifetimes.

Create Value through Customization

One of our main priorities is to mitigate the risks associated with your financial picture. The risk of market volatility (stock and bond markets) is on our minds with every prospective client we meet. This example portfolio offers good diversification, but there is still a high amount of traditional asset classes in the portfolio. A common recommendation would be to use non-correlated assets to reduce stock market volatility while still maintaining long-term performance opportunity. The institutional mindset of pension plans, endowments and wealthy investors come into play at this moment. What would they do in this scenario? Hint - read Chapter Six again to refresh your memory. With clients in their sixties, a drop in their portfolio value at a time when they are using their assets can be devastating, so the education regarding alternative asset classes becomes vital at this point in our discussion.

Next we tackle the concerns about inflation as a risk to one's personal economy. Every client needs to determine the impact a possible increasing interest rate environment would have on their current holdings. Ask yourself this question - do bonds still fit in your portfolio the same way they have for the last 10-20-30 years? You may desire to incorporate savings and investment vehicles that provide a natural hedge against inflation's effects on your financial picture or provide some type of income stream to *stay ahead* of inflation. Both the devaluation of our dollar and the potential increase in interest rates will arise as real inflation surfaces in the economy. Pinpointing which asset classes are a fit for your personal economy is key because your lifestyle needs and big ticket items may fluctuate in price as time goes on. Having access to a team of financial professionals that understand both the true definition of inflation and how to mitigate its devastating impact on your purchasing power can make a huge difference regarding your financial future.

Should you be worried about your income tax situation in the future? After all, most Americans have benefited greatly from tax-deferred contributions into 401k/IRA plans while they were accumulating their wealth. Our example has 70 percent of their liquid net worth in tax deferred accounts. Based on my 18 years of experience, that figure is representative of the majority of clients we serve but it's not uncommon to work with someone who has 80 to 90 percent of their wealth in tax deferred accounts. When someone begins accessing any of their investment accounts, the conversation about income taxes gets very real.

As you enter (or prepare to enter) the *distribution* phase of your life, the rules of money change drastically. You will want to choose strategies that keep your *effective* tax rate as low as possible each year. Our example has a current marginal federal tax bracket of 25 percent plus their state taxes. This could be lower in retirement (initially) by focusing on the *liquidation order* of their assets. The client could choose to *spend down* taxable assets that have a lower tax associated with them (capital gains at 15 percent vs. ordinary income at the 25 percent marginal level). It is even possible to reduce the amount of taxes paid on your social security income by managing your liquidation order of your assets. This is one reason that our firm has a social security/medicare specialist on staff to meet with any of our clients (at no cost) to assess their personal economy. You might decide to delay taking social security benefits or start receiving one spouse's benefits and delay the others. One thing I know for certain is that all of these decisions cannot be made in vacuum! While you may create some tax benefits early in your retirement, the *tax monster* growing inside of your tax deferred accounts must be dealt with at some point.

Required minimum distributions (RMDs) will start at age 70½. In this example, RMDs could amount to $30,000/yr. (conservative estimate) if the client chooses to wait and withdraw money from IRAs until they are forced to by the IRS. However, once you get to this point, you have backed yourself into "a corner" and essentially tied your tax professional's hands behind their backs. There is nothing that can be done to reduce your future tax liabilities because the RMD withdrawals will continue to increase as you get older and you do a good job of growing your account balances. So, how does someone pro-actively take control of their financial picture in this situation?

The key is to prioritize proper tax diversification strategies and balance your liquid net worth amongst taxable, tax-deferred, and tax-exempt financial vehicles. Even though you may not *need* to take money out of taxable and tax deferred accounts, you may *want* to make strategic distributions now. Pay the taxes on the money *once* and then re-position the after-tax funds into a tax exempt vehicle for future use. If you consider what possible changes to the capital gains and ordinary income tax rates the IRS could make in the future, having more money that is tax free will provide you more flexibility, access and control of your personal economy. After all, do you think tax rates will go down, stay the same or go up in the future? Your answer can help guide you to find a financial firm that understands your mindset.

While every client's situation is unique, there are steps we recommend for most clients to follow in order to accomplish the right amount of financial freedom. The most common strategies are listed below:
☐ Create an income plan that provides flexibility, liquidity, and control to cover your lifestyle (month-to-month) expenses and your big-ticket items (home improvements, autos, travel, children/grandchildren, toys, health care, emergencies).
☐ Work in tandem with a financial advisor or firm with knowledge on alternative asset classes along with a tax professional that can educate you on ways to "settle up" on your taxes from asset distributions without disturbing the rest of your tax picture
☐ Understand which alternative asset classes are a fit for your personal economy. Make sure that the risks of market volatility, inflation and taxes are addressed and the characteristics of safety, liquidity, and growth are present to the level you desire.
☐ Build a relationship with your team of financial professionals that is based on pro-active communication and transparency. Make sure they can manage your expectations and continue to adjust strategies as life events unfold that you were not expecting

The last risk I want to briefly mention is longevity – the concern of running out of money. Are you worried about running out of money? If you look at our example, based on our analysis and their current financial needs, this risk is not a high priority... *today.* But since no one has control over how an investment portfolio will perform in the future, what safeguards can anyone put in place to protect the purposes of their money? With defined benefits like pensions and social security, the longevity risk is on the corporation, financial institution or government providing the benefits. In today's society, those types of benefits are disappearing and individuals, families and entrepreneurs are scrambling to figure out ways to protect against the unexpected fear of "living too long." It is at this point in most discussions with clients, that I remind them why insurance companies exist. Insurance companies are in the business of *risk mitigation* and the good ones are very successful at figuring out ways to help their clients *transfer their biggest risks* to the insurance company for a cost. When it comes to retirement and income tax strategies, insurance companies have various annuity and life insurance contracts available to the public that allow the longevity risk to be transferred to their balance sheet. If you work with a financial professional who understands how these financial vehicles *complement* other traditional and alternative asset classes, then you can feel confident about enjoying your retirement years.

I bring this information to the reader's attention because there is a lack of education in today's society on how annuity and insurance contracts can be customized to fit your utilization strategies. Part of this reality is the fault of the insurance companies themselves because they operate in a world where most of their products are "sold" by licensed agents that are limited in their knowledge on many other financial solutions. This gives the public the mindset that agents just sell these financial vehicles for the *commissions*, not because the product is in the best interest of the client. There is also another side to the story; one where financial institutions are more focused on *risk taking* by the public to earn fees. The investment world has product sponsors, brokerage firms and asset managers that want you to believe the only way to grow your wealth is to put your money in the market. They want to *manage your risk*, not look for ways to reduce or mitigate it. Those firms will earn management fees and commissions when you put your monies into investment products available to them through their company or their firm's investment committee. The more assets they gather, the greater their revenue from fees. Of course, the public has the choice to purchase investment products on their own through "no load" vehicles but if a client desires expertise in the areas of financial strategies, that expertise will need to come from a professional and they will earn a fee for their service.

My point is simple: when you are attempting to find a financial advisor or firm to build a trusting, long term relationship, I encourage you to seek out someone or some place that creates value through their purpose, process, and philosophy; not based on the financial vehicles they can access. One of the advantages my firm, E3 Consultants Group, has over many of our competitors in the industry is that our business model was created with the notion that if we have access to almost any financial vehicle that is available to the public, all we need to do is educate them on our process and philosophy. If there's an agreement that we can add value to someone's financial picture, it will happen because customized solutions are implemented. That type of relationship with a client is what I want our readers to experience and expect in their personal economies!

A Message to all of the Entrepreneurs

In the last section of this chapter, I want to communicate directly to anyone who owns and operates a small business or those individuals who think entrepreneurially. When I say "small business," I mean a business that is privately held (not publicly traded), no matter the size of the company. The ownership of a small business is concentrated in a handful of people. These types of companies are the lifeblood of our economy and employ the majority of Americans. What is amazing to me is the *lack of support* these companies receive in our economic system due to the actions of the iron triangle (government, large corporations, and unions).

Understanding this reality was a big reason that I wrote this book. Also, my passion to work with like-minded, entrepreneurial people drives me to expand the message at the core of my company's existence—*to educate, empower, and enlighten the entrepreneur in all of us*—so that you, too, can achieve financial freedom.

What are the real concerns today for small business owners?

Cash Flow Management

We are experiencing historically low yields on cash reserves. What do you do with your cash? Let it sit in the bank? Put it to work for you and sacrifice liquidity?

Access to Credit

Banks have the capacity to loan out money, but they don't want to take any risks these days. What are your options? Take on new partners? Offer private equity? Use your own cash?

Economic Uncertainty

Because of our uncertain economy, true entrepreneurs these days find it difficult to keep the grow-or-die mentality unless they go it alone. Expansion options not only depend on your industry and opportunities but also on your capabilities for financing the new commitments while continuing to support your existing business model.

Employee Benefits

The cost of providing benefits can hamstring a business if there is no cost-control component. It can also hurt if they aren't incentivizing employees. You also must navigate the uncertainty of new government regulations and legislation on health care, disability, sick pay, bonuses, flex time, and more.

Executive Compensation

You want to attract and keep top talent for the best impact on your business. You also need to do succession planning to secure your company's legacy.

What do I know about business owners' personal economies?

I believe for many entrepreneurs, the best investment you can make with your money is to reinvest it back into your business. Why is this true?

It offers you *flexibility*: you know your business better than anyone else. Investing in a small business is really about having confidence in your abilities, knowledge, and creativity to add value in people's lives. Being able to make changes that protect your customers, your employees, and your family is essential in today's economic climate.

It also offers *accessibility*. Where does the highest return on your money come from? The bank? A brokerage account? Your 401k? No! It's *your business*.

If you are running a successful business, reinvesting more capital should create:

- Increased revenue that goes right to your bottom line (profit)
- Liquidity to fund expansion projects without relying on financial institutions
- The ability to grow your net worth by focusing on assets and not liabilities

What it really offers you, though, is *control*. The buck stops with you, so minimizing the risks that impact your business on a daily basis is vital. You don't want to just run a business that survives but rather *build* a business that thrives.

We understand your mindset and how you make decisions because we are small business owners, just like you.

How E3 Wealth's Advance-and-Protect Philosophy Could Make a Difference for Your Small Business

E3 Wealth will work with you to customize strategies that seek to minimize your risk in key areas that impact your business:

The Market & Economy

Our economy is still struggling to bounce back from the Great Recession. We have a slow housing recovery, an anemic job market, and flat real GDP growth. You cannot control what happens with this economy, but you can control how you respond to economic changes to minimize the impact on your company and its future. We can provide you continual education on how to maneuver your business through these tough economic times.

Taxes

With $17 trillion in US debt and a budget that spends 40 percent more than what comes in, where do you think taxes are headed in the future? Being a small business owner in the United States offers tremendous opportunity to build a lifestyle that few people will enjoy, and paying the least amount of taxes must be an integral part of your business plans. You are only required to pay taxes on your money once so why not implement strategies that help you accomplish that goal?

Inflation

As our currency continues to depreciate, your business feels the impact of inflation as the cost of raw materials increases and your profits dwindle. At the same time, your customers and clients will see their lifestyles eroding as prices go up. Inflation is another "hidden tax" on your small business that must be hedged so you can continue to grow.

Longevity

You started your business to create a livelihood for your family. Over time, it grows and becomes not just a place where you get a paycheck but rather an entity that creates jobs, services, and products—one that will leave a legacy long after you are gone. How you transition your business is key to its future existence. Succession planning, exit strategies, and retirement solutions are unique to each business and must be handled with care by professionals who can address your specific needs. After all, you have worked hard your whole life to get to this point.

Our integrated resource network is ready to serve all your financial needs. Our team of financial professionals specializes in several vital areas:

- Accounting, tax preparation, and tax strategies*
- Investment management
- Life insurance solutions
- Cash flow strategies (for month-to-month expenses and big-ticket items)
- Debt management
- Estate and succession planning
- Health and long-term care insurance resources
- Social Security and Medicare resources
- Economist and business consultant on retainer
- Business coach who teaches the science of NLP
                    (* NPC does not provide tax advice)

So how do successful investors or business owners operate their financial homes like a business? Check out the presentation in the appendix section of the book to expand your knowledge on this subject.

Conclusion

Well, we're at the end. Looking back on our journey in this book, first we diagnosed some of the problems Americans face because of the way people think, communicate, and behave regarding finance and money-related decisions. I wanted to open your eyes to the economic forces that inhibit most Americans from achieving financial security.

Then we touched on the difficult financial decisions that accompany each stage of life. Awareness that you are not alone in your questions and concerns about the direction of our society can be very empowering. Next, I outlined the resources available to you (and anyone who is willing to make a commitment) on the road to financial freedom.

I then spoke of the entrepreneurial spirit in all of us. Why? Because I think it's about time for America to become educated, empowered, and enlightened regarding financial freedom. Learning about the concepts of first-generation wealth, thinking like the rich, and NLP—the study of excellence—are your first steps. I introduced the process and philosophy that have provided our clients a way to *take control of their financial pictures* while *protecting their personal economies.* I shared some examples that show how you can *operate your financial home like a successful business.*

At this point, I want to make something very clear. I do not believe that this book includes "everything you need to know" about finance and money-related decisions. Getting all that information is a process that everyone must go through separately, and the results will be very subjective. This book is intended as the foundation for a new tomorrow independent of reliance on the government, financial institutions, and corporations.

Now ask yourself this question: "Based on the information in this book, am I more aware of how *successful* people think, communicate, and behave when it comes to finance and money-related decisions?" If the answer is *yes* then your next step is to determine how you'll use this information for your benefit. Seek out financial professionals who can assist you in customizing solutions specific to your financial picture.

I appreciate you joining me on this journey, and I hope you enjoy your future as your entrepreneurial spirit burns brighter every day.

Educate. Empower. Enlighten.

APPENDIX

Operating a Successful Business

ADVANCE & PROTECT

Characteristics:

* Conservative Mindset
* Good Saving Habits
* Focus on Minimizing Risk

Everyone has two areas of focus with their money:

* Success in your Occupation, Career or Business
* Managing your Personal Finances (Month-to-Month Expenses and Big-Ticket Items)

Main Sources of Capital to Start a Business:

ADVANCE & PROTECT

Bank Loans
* Bank Structures an Immediate Repayment Plan
* This Is a Business Expense You Prioritize
* Principal and Interest Are Controlled by the Bank

Personal Assets
* "Invest" in a Better Opportunity
* Why Take the Risk?
    - Potential Is Greater than Traditional Asset Classes (Stocks/Bonds/Cash)
    - You Are in Control of Your Future

Creating Strong Cash Flow

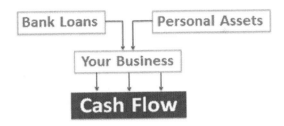

- Successful Businesses Create Strong, Positive Cash Flow that can be Reallocated however they choose

---

Reallocate Cash Flow to:

Accelerate Repayment of Bank Loans
- *Purpose:* Improve Financial Stability

Build Up Business Assets
- *Purpose:* Create Resources for **Big Ticket Items**
- *Examples:* Expansion, New Employees, Equipment, New Building, Marketing, Advertising, Technology, etc...
- *These Items should Cause Your Cash Flow to INCREASE and Improve Your Return on Investment (R.O.I)*

Build Up Personal Assets
- *Purpose:* Peace of Mind
- *Examples:* Purchase Autos, Kids' Education, Home Improvements, Travel, Healthcare, Other Business Opportunities...

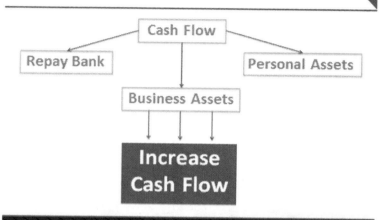

Opportunity Costs: ADVANCE
& PROTECT

Repay the Bank
* The Bank Controls More of Your Principal and the Terms of the Loan

Business Assets
* When You Pay Cash for Big Ticket Items, the Cash Stops Working for You

Personal Assets
* Re-Investment here normally flows back into Traditional Asset Classes (Bank, Mutual Funds, Brokerage Accounts)

Where Does Your Money "Sit"?

Repay the Bank
- These Funds Go to the Bank's Profit (Interest) and Replenish Their Loan Capabilities (Principal).

Business Assets
- Your Money Normally Sits in a Bank Account (Checking, Money Market, CD) Waiting for You to **USE IT**.

Personal Assets
- You Invest Your Money in Different Financial Institutions (Banks, Brokerage Firms, Mutual Funds, etc.).

Q: How Does a Successful Small Business Owner Minimize the Impact of Opportunity Costs on Their Financial Picture and Control the Flow of Their Money?

A: Consider a Different Financial Institution to hold your Cash Flow until you are ready to **USE IT**.

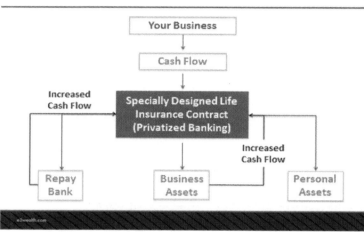

Components of a Specially Designed ADVANCE & PROTECT
Life Insurance Contract (S.D.L.I.C.)

- Mutual Insurance Company with Strong Financials

- Participating Whole Life Contracts with Design Flexibility

- A Contract that Allows Access to Cash Value through Policy Loans While You are Capitalizing the Policy

- A Contract that continues to Pay Dividends at the same level even though you are Using Your Own Money (Non-Direct Recognition)

Sources for Capitalization
(Building the Contract)

- Cash Flow
- Existing Business Assets in the Bank (Liquid)
- Existing Personal Assets (Liquid)

How to Capitalize a S.D.L.I.C.
- Fund/Capitalize the Contract over a 5-7 Year Period
- Optimize the Tax Benefits and Access to Cash Value much sooner this way.
- With some Companies, you can Access Part of Your Money within 30 Days of starting the Contract
- You can always continue Funding the Contract beyond the capitalization period

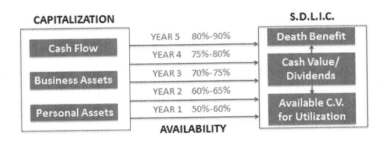

ADVANCE
& PROTECT

	New Capital	Policy Loans	Loan Payback
Dividends	⬆	SAME	SAME
Available C.V. for Loans	⬆	⬇	⬆
Death Benefit	⬆	⬇	⬆

Utilization Strategies (Cont.)

ADVANCE
& PROTECT

When You Borrow from the S.D.L.I.C.,

- It reduces what Cash Value you have available for Future Loans
- Your Death Benefit becomes Collateral for the Principal and Interest of the Loan
- Your Dividend is Not Affected by Utilizing Your Money and Increases Over Time

When You Pay Yourself Back

- Loan Repayments go towards Principal first and those payments are 100% Available for Future Use

Utilization Strategies (Cont.)

Key Points to Realize:
- Your Death Benefit could be 2.5x-5x your total New Capital (Based on Age and Health)
- You are building a solid foundation of Dividends that continue to grow throughout the Life of the Contract
- Borrowing from the contract does not affect the future growth of Guaranteed Cash Value or Dividends
- Borrowing does impact the access to available Cash Value for Future Loans - *A Finite Capacity that will Grow over time*

Utilization Strategies (Cont.)

Final Thoughts:
- This Concept Attempts to Replace the Way You Finance Your Big Ticket Purchases Throughout Your Life

- A S.D.L.I.C. is Not an Investment. It is a Financial Vehicle that Allows You to Minimize the Risks of Market Volatility, Inflation and Taxes While Capturing the Lost Opportunity Costs When You Use Your Money.

e3wealth.com